DANGEROUS
WATER CREATURES

The Encyclopedia of Danger

DANGEROUS ENVIRONMENTS

DANGEROUS FLORA

DANGEROUS INSECTS

DANGEROUS MAMMALS

DANGEROUS NATURAL PHENOMENA

DANGEROUS PLANTS AND MUSHROOMS

DANGEROUS PROFESSIONS

DANGEROUS REPTILIAN CREATURES

DANGEROUS SPORTS

DANGEROUS WATER CREATURES

CHELSEA HOUSE PUBLISHERS

The Encyclopedia of Danger

DANGEROUS
WATER CREATURES

Missy Allen

Michel Peissel

CHELSEA HOUSE PUBLISHERS

New York　　　　　Philadelphia

The Encyclopedia of Danger includes general information on treatment and prevention of injuries and illnesses. The publisher advises the reader to seek the advice of medical professionals and not to use these volumes as a first aid manual.

On the cover   Watercolor painting of a piranha by Michel Peissel

Chelsea House Publishers

Editor-in-Chief   Remmel Nunn
Managing Editor   Karyn Gullen Browne
Copy Chief   Mark Rifkin
Picture Editor   Adrian G. Allen
Art Director   Maria Epes
Assistant Art Director   Howard Brotman
Manufacturing Director   Gerald Levine
Systems Manager   Lindsey Ottman

The Encyclopedia of Danger
Editor   Karyn Gullen Browne

Staff for DANGEROUS WATER CREATURES
Assistant Editor   Martin Mooney
Production Editor   Marie Claire Cebrián
Designer   Diana Blume
Editorial Assistant   Karen Hirsch

First Printing

1 3 5 7 9 8 6 4 2

Library of Congress Cataloging-in-Publication Data

Peissel, Michel.
Dangerous water creatures/Michel Peissel, Missy Allen.
p. cm.—(The Encyclopedia of danger)
Includes bibliographical references and index.
Summary: Examines 24 dangerous animals found in the oceans, rivers, and lakes of the world, from the arctic jellyfish to the weever fish.
ISBN 0-7910-1788-5
1. Dangerous aquatic animals—Encyclopedias, Juvenile. [1. Dangerous aquatic animals. 2. Aquatic animals. 3. Dangerous animals.] I. Allen, Missy. II. Title.
III. Series: Peissel, Michel, Encyclopedia of danger.

QL100.P45 1992
591.6'5'0916—dc20
Printed in Mexico

91-39071
CIP
AC

CONTENTS

THE ENCYCLOPEDIA OF DANGER

"Mother Nature" is not always motherly; often, she behaves more like a wicked aunt than a nurturing parent. She can be unpredictable and mischievous—she can also be downright dangerous.

The word *danger* comes from the Latin *dominium*—"the right of ownership"—and Mother Nature guards her domain jealously indeed, using an ingenious array of weapons to punish trespassers. These weapons have been honed to a fatal perfection during millions of years of evolution, and they can be insidious or overwhelming, subtle or brutal. There are insects that spray toxic chemicals and insects that go on the march in armies a million strong; there are snakes that spit venom and snakes that smother the life from their victims; there are fish that inflict electric shocks and fish that can strip a victim to the bones; there are even trees that exude poisonous gases and flowers that give off a sweet—and murderous—perfume.

Many citizens of the modern, urban, or suburban world have lost touch with Mother Nature. This loss of contact is dangerous in itself; to ignore her is to invite her wrath. Every year, hundreds of children unknowingly provoke her anger by eating poisonous berries or sucking deadly leaves or roots; others foolishly cuddle toxic toads or step on venomous sea creatures. Naive travelers expose themselves to a host of unsuspected natural dangers, but you do not have to fly to a faraway country to encounter one of Mother Nature's sentinels; many of them can be found in your own apartment or backyard.

The various dangers featured in these pages range from the domestic to the exotic. They can be found throughout the world, from the deserts to the polar regions, from lakes and rivers to the depths of the oceans, from subterranean passages to high mountaintops, from rainforests to backyards, from barns to bathrooms. Which of these dangers are the most dangerous? We have prepared a short list of 10 of the most formidable weapons in Mother Nature's arsenal:

Grizzly bear.   Undoubtedly one of the most ferocious creatures on the planet, the grizzly needs little provocation to attack, maul, and maybe even eat a person. (There is something intrinsically more terrifying about an animal that will not only kill you but eat you—and not necessarily in that order—as well.) Incredibly strong, a grizzly can behead a moose with one swipe of its paw. Imagine what it could do to *you.*

Cape buffalo.   Considered by many big-game hunters to be the most evil-tempered animal in all of Africa, cape-buffalo bulls have been known to toss a gored body—perhaps the body of an unsuccessful big-game hunter—around from one pair of horns to another.

Weever fish.   The weever fish can inflict a sting so agonizing that victims stung on the finger have been known to cut off the finger in a desperate attempt to relieve the pain.

Estuarine crocodile.   This vile human-eater kills and devours an estimated 2,000 people annually.

Great white shark.   The infamous great white is a true sea monster. Survivors of great white shark attacks—and survivors are rare—usually face major surgery, for the great white's massive jaws inflict catastrophic wounds.

Army ants.   Called the "Genghis Khans of the insect world" by one entomologist, army ants can pick an elephant clean in a few days and routinely cause the evacuation of entire villages in Africa and South America.

Blue-ringed octopus.   This tentacled sea creature is often guilty of over-kill; it frequently injects enough venom into the wound of a single human victim to kill ten people.

Introduction

Black widow spider. The female black widow, prowler of crawl spaces and outhouses, produces a venom that is 15 times as potent as rattlesnake poison.

Lorchel mushroom. Never make a soup from these mushrooms—simply inhaling the fumes would kill you.

Scorpion. Beware the sting of this nasty little arachnid, for in Mexico it kills 10 people for every 1 killed by poisonous snakes.

DANGEROUS WATER CREATURES

Water is the essential medium for life on this planet; all earth's life-forms, including *Homo sapiens*, evolved from ocean-born organisms. Many of these organisms eventually left the oceans behind and developed into land-dwelling creatures, but the oceans—as well as the earth's rivers, streams, lakes, and ponds—still host a fabulous variety of aquatic life. Some of the oceanic life-forms included in *Dangerous Water Creatures* sound like fanciful creations from Jules Verne's *Twenty Thousand Leagues Under the Sea*: a tiny octopus whose sting is 99% fatal; moray eels, who were at one time accustomed to a steady diet of Roman slaves; the Portuguese man-of-war, whose sting is compared to being "struck by a bolt of lightning"; and the puffer fish, an essential ingredient in Voodoo potions. Freshwater curiosities are also included here: the tiny candiru, which has a weird and entirely unpleasant affinity for the human urethra; the garfish, whose skin is so tough it can withstand a projectile fired from a powerful spear gun; and the electric catfish, which has such a quarrelsome (and shocking) disposition that it cannot be kept in an aquarium with other fish.

In order to study the often bewildering variety of life on earth, naturalists developed a system of classification that divides the animal kingdom into major groups, which in turn are divided into subgroups, then sub-subgroups, and so on. The phyla comprise the first major categories. A single phylum consists of several classes; a class is divided into orders; an order is made up of different families; a family has various branches called genera; and a genus (the singular of genera) has subdivisions called species. Species is the most exact category; animals belonging to the same species are the most closely related. For example, two animals belonging to the same phylum might be described as very distant biological cousins, whereas animals of the same species are more like biological brothers and sisters. Here is a brief overview of the phyla discussed in *Dangerous Water Creatures*:

Phylum: Chordata

The Chordata phylum is one of the most varied in the animal kingdom. Its members (chordates) include microscopic tunicates, fish, reptiles, birds, mammals, and humans. The chordates discussed in *Dangerous Water Creatures* are fish and reptiles.

Fish are any of 30,000 species of cold–blooded aquatic vertebrates (having a spinal column). They are the most primitive of all earth's vertebrates, having arisen 500 million years ago. They use gills to breathe and fins to propel themselves. Fish vary greatly in size, shape, and color; the Philippine Island goby is 1/3 of an inch long, whereas the whale shark measures 50 feet in length.

Reptiles are considered to be the evolutionary link between marine and land animals. Most reptiles have become well adapted to life on land, but some, such as sea turtles and sea snakes, have developed in such a way that they are best suited to a marine environment.

Phylum: Coelenterata

The members of the Coelenterata phylum (coelenterates), which includes jellyfish and sea anemones, are almost all marine invertebrates (lacking a spinal column) found primarily along the shores of warm saltwater seas. All coelenterates have a centrally located mouth surrounded by whorls of tentacles, which are studded with nematocysts (stinging cells).

Phylum: Echinodermata

The echinoderms, including starfish, sand dollars, sea urchins, and sea cucumbers, are exclusively aquatic. Most echinoderms are bottom dwellers that thrive in warm, shallow waters, but some are common to deep and colder waters. Most echinoderms are symmetrical in shape, with five regular body parts arranged around a center.

Phylum: Molluska

The mollusks compose a phylum of typically hard–shelled sea creatures that includes oysters, clams, snails, slugs, squid, and octopuses. Mollusks have been around for 600 million years. The physiology of mollusks is characterized by the mantle, or body wall, that bears shell-secreting glands, and the radula, a toothy food–grasping organ. Most mollusks are small, although some can be quite large. Squid can grow as long as 60 feet in length.

Phylum: Porifera

The poriferans are sponges—multicellular invertebrates without tissue or true organs. Sponges attach themselves to fixed objects in the water and ingest oxygen and nutrients from the water as it passes through their porous body cavity.

KEY

HABITAT

FOREST

SEA

WOOD/TRASH

TOWNS

SHORE

GRASS/FIELDS

MOUNTAINS

SWAMP/MARSH

GARDEN

FRESH WATER

JUNGLE

BUILDING

DESERT

KEY

HOW IT GETS PEOPLE

INGESTION

TOUCH

STING

BITE

SPIT

SPRAY

MAUL

CLIMATIC ZONE

TEMPERATE

TROPICAL

ARCTIC

MORTALITY

ONE

TWO

THREE

FOUR

13

ARCTIC JELLYFISH

HOW IT GETS PEOPLE

Cyanea capillata

HABITAT

CLIMATIC ZONE

CLIMATIC ZONE

RATING

General

In the cold green depths of the Arctic Ocean lurks an animal more than 200 feet long and composed almost entirely of water. Shaped like a gelatinous bell, the arctic jellyfish is sometimes broader than a man is tall, and its drapery of stinging tentacles trailing beneath the bell can sweep an area larger than a basketball court. Its size, shape, and dangerous tentacles have given it the nicknames "lion's mane," "sea blubber," and "medusa."

Jellyfish, sometimes called by their generic name, *Cyanea*, get progressively smaller the farther south they are found. In the waters off the Carolinas, for instance, they are only the size of saucers. This phenomenon may occur because cold seas have vaster concentrations of life than do warm seas and abound with small crustaceans and fish. Perhaps arctic jellyfish are gargantuan because they have more to eat.

14

Arctic Jellyfish

Like other jellyfish, the arctic variety has up to 1,200 tentacles, which are bunched into eight clusters and are packed with millions of nematocysts, or stinging cells. Each of these nematocysts contains a tiny venomous harpoon that shoots out to stun a potential food source or an imposing enemy.

This jellyfish even played the villain in Sir Arthur Conan Doyle's *Adventure of the Lion's Mane*. The brilliant detective Sherlock Holmes is mystified by the sudden seaside death of a science teacher known to have a history of heart trouble. Holmes unearths the culprit, a very large jellyfish. "Cyanea," cries Holmes, "behold the Lion's Mane." Although there are no official reports of arctic jellyfish fatalities, it is certainly possible that a swimmer, especially one with a history of heart trouble, could go into shock and drown after being stung by one of these beasts.

Name/Description

The arctic jellyfish (*Cyanea capillata*) is the largest jellyfish in the world. Bluish, reddish, or brown, it consists of immensely long tentacles attached to a bloated body six to seven feet in diameter. The upper surface

of the body disk is circular, almost flat, and roughened. Umbrella shaped, its tentacles are bunched into eight clusters that hang from its upper body. The arctic jellyfish, like most others, swims by rhythmic pulsations that indeed resemble an umbrella being slowly opened and shut. The body of a jellyfish is coordinated by a very simple nervous system and by sense organs around the edge of the upper surface of its body that respond to light, gravity, and chemicals in the water.

Highly resilient as long as it is in water, the jellyfish is doomed if stranded onshore. Composed 98% of water, a jellyfish will quickly evaporate under the hot rays of the sun, leaving little more than a wet spot in the sand. Carnivorous, they feed on fish, shrimp, and other sea animals that come into contact with their deadly tentacles.

Toxicology

Victims are stung by the nematocysts on the tentacles. Essentially little oval capsules, the nematocysts house a coiled, pointed, and hollow thread bathed in poison. When the thread comes into contact with prey, a hairlike trigger projects from the capsule and shoots out of the thread like a tiny harpoon. If the harpoon penetrates, it can inject venom. The poison is thought to be neurotoxic, which means that it affects the conduction or transmission of nerve impulses.

Symptoms

The first symptoms are immediate pain and a stinging sensation. There will be wheals (welts) and redness where the tentacles touched the skin. Then there will be difficulty in respiration, frothing at the mouth, and loss of consciousness.

Treatment

Vinegar, methylated spirits, or diluted acetic acid should be poured over any remaining clinging tentacles to inhibit further venomous discharge.

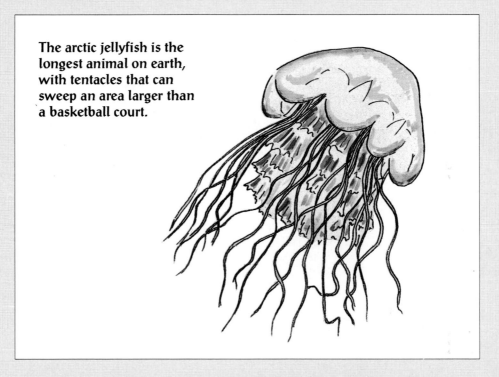

The arctic jellyfish is the longest animal on earth, with tentacles that can sweep an area larger than a basketball court.

Also, drying agents, such as talcum powder, should be applied to the skin before attempting to pull out the threads. The affected extremity should be elevated. Rubbing or scratching the affected area may discharge unreleased nematocysts that will inevitably be present on the skin. The victim may also need to be treated for shock (see Bites, Gorings, Maulings, and Shock, p. 112).

BARRACUDA

HOW IT GETS PEOPLE

Genus: Sphyraena

HABITAT

HOW IT GETS PEOPLE

CLIMATIC ZONE

CLIMATIC ZONE

RATING

General

What creature of the deep is so vicious that, according to marine scientists Herald and Vogt, many divers in tropical regions fear their attacks more than they fear sharks? Sometimes called the "tigers of the sea," barracuda are handsome, fearless killers that hunt by sight. Bright colors or unusual movements, such as those of an injured fish or a panicky diver, are more than sufficient to attract a roving barracuda. In murky water, a barracuda might have difficulty distinguishing between the two and go after the less tasty diver. Scientists contend that, in clear water, humans have little to fear from a barracuda attack. But surely Pablo Bush Romero, the doyen of Mexican skin divers, would disagree. He tells of a man who had the flesh stripped off one leg by a barracuda

18

Barracuda

while standing in only a foot of water off the coast of Quintana Roo, in the Yucatán Peninsula, not a unique incident in that area.

When presented with a barracuda in the water, potential victims are cautioned to stay still, which seems completely unnatural when faced with such a terrifying predator. One can imagine how difficult it would be for a diver to try to stay motionless as long as possible with a giant barracuda circling around, baring its razor-sharp teeth. However, to try swimming away would be prove futile for two reasons. First, the barracuda is one of the fastest-swimming fish in the sea and has been clocked at more than 27 miles per hour. (Humans have been clocked at 5 MPH.) Second, in a recent study on sharks and barracuda it was concluded that jerky, rapid movements—such as those made by a panicky human trying to swim away—releases the attack pattern in barracuda. The study went on to say that when people act smoothly and calmly, the pattern is not released.

Barracuda is one species that is almost as dangerous on the dinner table as it is in the water. Eating barracuda can be dangerous because certain species in the Atlantic feed on the toxic puffer fish (see p. 66), thus making their own flesh poisonous. In 1982, on the island of Bimini in the

Bahamas, 15 sailors were hospitalized—several in critical condition—from eating barracuda.

Name/Description

Barracuda belong to any of 18 species of the one genus, *Sphyraena*, of the family Sphraenidae. They have long, slender, muscular bodies covered with cycloid, or circular, scales. Their heads are large and pointed. Sharp, conical teeth line the jaws and the palatine bone; the longer teeth are used for seizing prey, and the daggerlike, backward-curving teeth are used mainly for cutting and shredding. Their diet consists primarily of sardines. It is the larger barracuda, known as the Great Barracuda (*Sphyraena barracuda*), that attacks humans. This species has been measured at six to eight feet long and weighs more than 100 pounds.

Injury

Because barracuda hunt by sight, it is thought that attacks on humans are cases of mistaken identity. (Barracuda, like most other predators of the deep, would probably rather eat other fish than humans.) It seems that barracuda are attracted by flashy, metallic, or multicolored clothing and gear, which can easily be mistaken for the underbelly of a fish. Fortunately, they usually make only a single attack, which in most instances is not fatal, though mutilations and amputations are not uncommon. Although a barracuda bite might take off a limb or a large chunk of flesh, it usually produces a clean wound (unlike the ragged-edged wounds produced by sharks). See Bites, Gorings, Maulings, and Shock, p. 112.

Treatment

It is urgent to control blood loss because the victim can easily go into shock and die. If absolutely necessary (such as in the case of an open

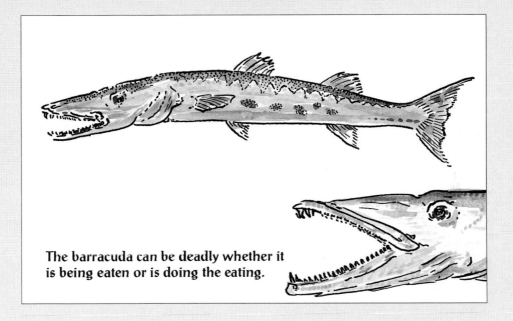

The barracuda can be deadly whether it is being eaten or is doing the eating.

artery), a tourniquet may be applied. Use a compression bandage on an oozing wound.

Prevention

- Bathing and diving wear and gear should be as simple and dark as possible.
- Areas where barracuda are known to habitate should be avoided, especially if the water is murky.
- When confronted by a barracuda, one should stay as still as possible. It is foolish to try and swim away from it.

BLUE-RINGED OCTOPUS

HOW IT GETS PEOPLE

Hapolochlaena maculosa, H. lunata, and H. fasciata

HABITAT

CLIMATIC ZONE

RATING

General

Deaths from octopus bites were long rumored, but it was only within the last quarter century that the culprit, the blue-ringed octopus, was identified. The less than half-dozen species of this minute creature have blue rings that, when excited, become iridescent. Although all octopuses are potentially venomous, the blue-ringed octopus is the only one that has proven fatal to humans. It first bites its victim with its parrotlike beak and then spits deadly venom into the tiny puncture wound. Blue-ringed octopus venom is so potent that scientists at the Commonwealth Serum Laboratories in Melbourne, Australia, claim that the amount secreted through the horny beak at one time is sufficient to kill 10 people.

Probably the best-documented blue-ringed octopus attack was that experienced by Kirke Dyson-Holland, a 21-year-old skin diver who was

Blue-Ringed Octopus

bitten off East Point, near Darwin, Australia. His diving companion, John Baylis, caught what he thought was a harmless little octopus, played with it, and then tossed it to Dyson–Holland. The animal sat on Dyson–Holland's shoulder for a minute before crawling onto the middle of his back and dropping off. Forgetting the tiny creature, the two men went ashore. As soon as Dyson–Holland reached the shore, he became violently ill. Baylis saw the puncture marks and rushed him to a hospital, where Dyson–Holland died less than two hours after being bitten. Because the victim had a history of asthma and at least one allergy, allergic reaction was thought to have caused his death. That was until Private James Arthur Ward—in perfect health, as he had been inducted into the Australian army two days earlier—was bitten by a four-inch blue-ringed octopus and died within 90 minutes.

From these accounts it should be obvious that playing with small octopuses, especially in the western Pacific, can be deadly. But even a seemingly harmless activity such as seashell collecting has proved perilous because shells are one of their favorite hiding places. In one incident, an Australian diver stuck inside his wet suit a beautiful conch

shell with a stowaway blue-ringed octopus. But he was lucky and was rushed by helicopter to a hospital before paralysis set in.

The only compensation for blue-ringed octopus envenomization is that it is quick. As Clyde Roper, a marine researcher in Australia, explains, "It bites, and you don't feel it. You get numb. Then you find it hard to talk. Then paralysis sets in, but you remain conscious. Then you have respiratory failure, and about two hours after the bite . . . zingo."

Name/Description

Blue-ringed octopuses are tiny cephalopod mollusks. Only four to six inches long, they have eight muscular arms, each equipped with two rows of suckers. Species described here are *Hapolochlaena maculosa*, which are also known as *Octopus maculosa*; *H. lunata*, also known as *O. rugosus*; and *H. fasciata*. Their common name derives from the bright blue rings that cover their entire body. At rest, the blue-ringed octopus has brown or ocher bands over its body and arms, with blue circles superimposed on these bands. When aroused, these bands darken and the blue rings appear to light up until they are an iridescent peacock blue.

Toxicology

To envenom, the blue-ringed octopus bites with its beak, leaving two tiny puncture wounds into which it spits venom brought down from its salivary glands. Although the chemical action of venom is not fully understood, it apparently affects the conductivity of the nerves and the junctions where nerve and muscle meet, causing failure of all voluntary muscular activity. It is thought that there may be an anticoagulant (a substance that prevents the blood from clotting) constituent in the venom because profuse bleeding has been reported in some cases.

Symptoms

A blue-ringed octopus bite leaves two small puncture wounds, but there is no initial pain. Within minutes there is a dryness and numbness of the

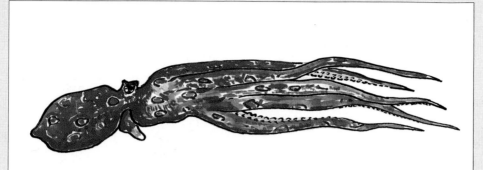

A single bite from the blue-ringed octopus contains enough venom to kill 10 people.

mouth and throat and difficulty in swallowing, followed by vomiting, loss of muscular control, failing eyesight, and paralysis, which usually begins near the site of the bite and spreads to all parts of the body. Death comes from respiratory failure as a result of paralysis of the diaphragm muscles.

Treatment

Blue–ringed octopus venom acts incredibly fast, so getting the victim to a doctor quickly is paramount to his or her recovery. There is no specific treatment and no known antivenin (antitoxin to venom). A doctor may administer oxygen and adrenalin and may place the victim on an artificial respirator.

Prevention

- Refrain from swimming in areas inhabited by blue-ringed octopuses.
- Never handle or even approach a small octopus in the western Pacific.
- Be cautious when collecting shells—they could be harboring a stowaway.

CANDIRU

CLIMATIC ZONE

Vandellia cirrhosa

HABITAT

HOW IT GETS PEOPLE

HOW IT GETS PEOPLE

RATING

General

When Professor C. H. Eigenmann of Indiana University, on a trip to the Amazon region in the early 20th century, noticed some of the native peoples donning strange codpieces (a flap or bag covering the groin) before entering the water, he took note. After inquiring about this practice, he was told of an animal that attacked humans in the most sensitive area of their body. His reports were met with less than universal belief. It was not until 1930, when Eugene W. Cudger wrote his article "Candiru, the Only Vertebrate Predator of Man," that the candiru was elevated from jungle lore to scientific fact.

Candiru

Found almost exclusively in the deep, dark waters of the Amazon River of South America, the candiru, a minute parasitic catfish, has a bizarre affinity for human urethras (the membranous canal through which urine is discharged from the bladder). Normally, these tiny fish live in the gills and urethralike chambers of larger fish. But these lilliputian creatures also enter the urethra of unsuspecting bathers, particularly if these humans happen to urinate in the water. The candiru has weak eyes, and in the murky waters of the Amazon it is forced to hunt not by sight but by smell. It is thought that they mistake the flow of human urine for the exhalant stream of water from a fish's gills, their preferred habitat.

The only vertebrate to parasitize humans and the only parasite of the entire fish group, candirus have an equal affinity for the urogenital apertures of both men and women. Entering the urethra like a worm going into its burrow, they immediatcly erect the retrorse (backward-pointing) spines on their gill covers. These spines serve two important functions: First, they start a blood flow on which the candiru feeds; and second, the spines hold them securely in place. The pain, as one might

27

suspect, is said to be spectacular. Once in place, there is no way a candiru can be removed without surgical intervention. And even then a victim runs a great risk of blood poisoning. Unfortunately, there is not adequate medical care available for such victims in the Amazon region, and many Indian men have had to undergo primitive amputations to prevent the parasite from reaching the bladder. This horrendous treatment has led to the custom of covering one's genitalia and lower torso with protective sheaths made from palm fibers.

Name/Description

The candiru (*Vandellia cirrhosa*) is a very small (two inches long) South American parasitic catfish that is known there as the "carnero." Long and slim like a matchstick, it penetrates and lives in the gill chambers and cloacae (common passages for fecal, urinary, and reproductive discharge) of larger fish. Once inside the fish, it erects sharp retrorse spines on its gill covers. These spines keep it firmly anchored in place and induce a blood flow on which it feeds.

Injury

Aside from the risk of infection from the spines, the mere presence of the candiru can lead to blood poisoning as well.

Symptoms

The erection of the spines and the sharp bites of the candiru produce immediate excruciating pain.

Treatment

The only treatment is surgical intervention to remove the fish.

Candiru

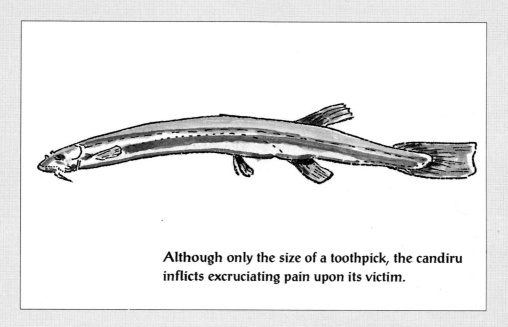

Although only the size of a toothpick, the candiru inflicts excruciating pain upon its victim.

Prevention

- In the Amazonian regions where the candiru is found, the native peoples cover their genitalia—either with their hands or protective sheaths made of palm fibers—when entering the water.

CONE SHELL

HOW IT GETS PEOPLE

Genus: Conus

HABITAT

CLIMATIC ZONE

RATING

General

How can something so beautiful and fragile–looking be so fatal? Cone shells are among the most prized acquisitions of discriminating shell collectors. One species, the "glory of the seas" (*Conus gloriamaris*), has fetched prices in the thousands of dollars.

Cone shells may bring glorious prices, but they are as dangerous as they are attractive, and their suborder name, Toxglossa, or "poison tongue," seems much more appropriate. The poison is not really in a tongue but in tiny harpoonlike structures known as radular teeth, which are hollow and are connected to the venom source. The cone shell uses them to stun and capture small fish. Once its prey is stilled, the cone slides over it and engulfs it with its highly extendable mouth.

Much too tiny to engulf a human victim, cone shells can nonetheless inflict a fatal sting. This ability has earned them a danger rating of two in the *United States Navy Diving Manual*, putting them on a par with, among other killers, lemon sharks.

30

Cone Shell

The cone shell has a long history of inflicting serious and fatal stings. In 1705, a slave on the Banda Islands, in Indonesia, was hauling nets along the beach. Mixed in with her squirming catch was a beautiful textile cone, *C. textile.* What happened next is not certain. She may have picked it up, grabbed it, or even just brushed against it. In any event, she died a short time later. The episode was witnessed by the Dutch naturalist G. E. Rumphius, who gave the literature of Europe its first eyewitness account of cone shell envenomization.

In Japan, Kamekichi Fujisato went to the beach to swim and to collect seashells. Fujisato had just picked up a beautiful shell when he heard his companion shout a warning, but he was stung on the thumb before he could drop the shell. At first he felt no pain. But by the time he had walked the 120 yards to the road, he could not go any farther and rolled into a potato field. He was still conscious when the doctor arrived but Fujisato could hardly breathe. His pulse slowed, his body temperature fell, he lost consciousness, his extremities became purplish in color, and less than four hours later he died.

Cases of cone shell envenomization are numerous throughout the Asian seas. Although people are aware of the existence of them, they are

not cautious. Adding to the increase in the number of attacks are shell collectors' demands for live specimens combined with the ever-growing numbers of amateur divers.

Name/Description

There are perhaps 400 to 500 different multicolored species of cone shells of the genus *Conus*. Varying greatly in size from one to nine inches, they are divided basically into three groups, according to what they eat: the vermivorous species (worm eaters), piscivorous species (fish eaters), and the gastropod species, which eat other gastropods. Cone shells are most active near the shore, but only at high tide. Shy and retiring, many species hide under rocks or bury themselves in the sand. Often associated with coral reefs, they prefer shallow water and are found in isolated bays and in the inlets of remote islands. Their forward movement is inexorable and rather slow.

The cone shell's means of envenomization is unusual. Like arrows in a quiver, the radular teeth are stored in a sac. Each tooth is hollow and carries its own venom supply. When a cone shell prepares to strike, it positions its radular teeth to the tip of its muscular proboscis, which can extend several inches in all directions. The size of the darts and the amount of poison vary with the species, and there is no correlation between the size of the cone shell and the size of the dart.

Toxicology

There are indications that cone shell venom interferes with neuro-muscular transmission and that it is composed of a mixture of active substances, including protein quaternary ammonium compounds and possibly amines.

Symptoms

Symptoms range from a pain like the sensation of a bee sting to death within four or five hours. There will be blanching at the site of the

Although cone shells can be worth thousands of dollars, simply touching one can be fatal.

envenomization, cyanosis (discoloration of the skin as a result of lack of oxygen) of the surrounding area, numbness, a stinging or burning sensation, blurring of the vision, loss of speech, difficulty in swallowing, nausea, and extreme weakness. In more serious cases, coma or death (usually from respiratory paralysis or cardiac failure) may follow.

Treatment

There is no specific antidote for cone shell envenomization; it must be treated symptomatically.

Prevention

• It is best never to pick up anything that looks like a cone shell.

• Wear gloves when collecting shells.

ELECTRIC CATFISH

HOW IT GETS PEOPLE

Malapterusus electricus

RATING

CLIMATIC ZONE

HABITAT

HABITAT

General

A rather repulsive-looking creature, electric catfishes live in African rivers and lakes. Somewhat sluggish, it is thought that without their ability to discharge electric shocks to stun their prey they would have a hard time finding enough to eat. Voracious eaters, they will consume almost anything they can find, from worms to small fish. But because electric catfish have such quarrelsome dispositions, they cannot be kept in captivity: Hence, little is known of their other habits. When provoked, electric catfish make a strong initial discharge (up to 350 volts) followed by a succession of several lesser shocks. However, they tire easily and cannot keep up a sequence of discharges long enough to fatally injure a human.

Electric Catfish

Electricity is present in all living things and is linked with the very nature of living matter; every time a muscle is moved, a tiny electric current is involved in transmitting an impulse down a nerve to stimulate contraction of that muscle. Some of the electric catfish's muscles have lost their power to contract but have compensated for this disability with an increase in their electric power.

These mustached creatures were depicted in ancient Egyptian bas-reliefs and tomb paintings dating from 2750 B.C. Even earlier, from 4000 B.C., the electric catfish was known in hieroglyphics as "he who releases many"—the implication being that a fisher hauling in a net in which an electric catfish was caught would, on receiving a shock, drop the net and liberate the catch. Although the Egyptians were aware of its dangers, they ate electric catfish, as other Africans have done ever since.

In tropical Africa, electric catfish have been used as a remedy for aches and pains—a live electric catfish being placed over the painful area, giving the patient an electric shock. Arabs also have used the electric catfish, which they call "raad," meaning "thunder" or "shock," in this same type of electrotherapy since the 11th century.

Dangerous Water Creatures

Name/Description

The electric catfish (*Malapterusus electricus*) is a plump (up to 50 pounds), scaleless fish that lacks the sharp and sometimes poisonous spines on the dorsal and pectoral fins characteristic of most other catfish. Nocturnal, these fish have very small eyes. Their body is mottled with irregular black blotches, and their mouth bristles with three pairs of sensory barbels (the "whiskers" that give the catfish its name).

The electric organs are formed from modified muscle cells that lie just under the skin of the long (up to four feet) body and tail. The organs are divided into compartments containing electroplates, which are branched to a large nerve cell in the spinal cord.

Injury

Electric catfish are capable of producing electric discharges of up to 350 volts, which can easily stun a human and may render him or her unconscious.

Treatment

Lay the victim down and keep him or her calm; the effects will pass quickly. See also Bites, Gorings, Maulings, and Shock, p. 112.

Pharmacology

Arabs and Africans have long used electric catfish in a type of electrotherapy, applying them to painful areas of the body.

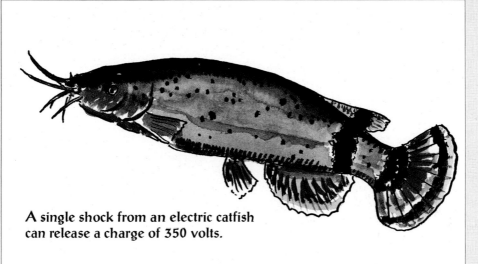

A single shock from an electric catfish
can release a charge of 350 volts.

Electric catfish have such a nasty disposition
that they cannot even be kept in captivity.

ELECTRIC EEL

HOW IT GETS PEOPLE

Electrophorous electricus

HABITAT

CLIMATIC ZONE

RATING

General

In 1800 the German baron Alexander von Humboldt received special permission from the Spanish government to travel freely throughout its South American colonies. Along with the famed French botanist Aimé Bonpland, Humboldt collected and studied the spectacular flora and fauna of the tropical rainforests of Venezuela, Colombia, and Peru; he also traveled through the Portuguese colony of Brazil. In Calabozo, a ranching station in Venezuela, Humboldt came across an eel that, when he accidentally stepped on it, gave him, as he described it, "a violent pain in the knees, and in almost every joint."

The renowned naturalist Humboldt discovered and gave the world the first scientific accounts of the electric eel. He concluded his study with the hypothesis that electricity is the source of life and movement in all living things—an astoundingly accurate hypothesis for a scientist to have made some 200 years ago. With obvious difficulty, Humboldt managed to obtain some specimens and make a detailed description of these serpentine fish and their powerful electric organs, which are capable of producing paralyzing discharges. (Humboldt collected specimens by using an Indian trick: The Indians native to the region would run animals, such as cows or horses, through electric-eel-infested water. The eels would discharge their electricity on the animals, leaving the water safe for the Indians until the eels could regenerate electricity. Humboldt, however, was the unlucky recipient of a shock from an eel that had not discharged all its juice.)

Unfortunately, in the century that followed Humboldt's discovery, interest in this new beast waned, and there is little mention of electric eels again until 1941. That year, an incredible scenario developed involving anti-Nazi Germans, scientists, the U.S. Army, and Amazonian Indians. Roger Caras, in his book, *Dangerous to Man*, explains:

Late in 1941, two native workers in the Brazilian state of Amazonas were walking on a plank stretched across a large cement pool. Nobody seems to know precisely how it happened, but one end of the plank slipped from its mooring and the two men fell into the water. They were killed instantly. The pool contained a number of electric eels, which had been requested by Dr. Christopher W. Coates, curator of the New York Aquarium, and Dr. David Nachmansohn, on assignment for the U.S.

Dangerous Water Creatures

Army Chemical Corps. The greater part of the research in which these doctors were engaged had to do with finding an antidote for the devastating nerve gas G developed in Germany in the 1930s. The whole episode with the electric eels, and their subsequent transport to the United States, appears to have been in the best tradition of a spy melodrama. Before it was over, at least one other man (an anti-Nazi German working on the project) was killed by the fish.

Able to kill a human on contact, electric eels have been known to knock out a horse crossing a stream from 20 feet away. They have also been known to emit powerful discharges eight to nine hours after their death. The largest discharge on record was that of a 90-pound electric eel at the Bronx Zoo in New York. It zapped an amazing 650 volts.

Name/Description

The electric eel *Electrophorous electricus* is not an eel but a fish of the family Gymnotidae. They are large (up to 6 1/2 feet long), sluggish, and sturdily built (they can weigh up to 45 pounds). About 85% of their body is the tail; the alimentary canal, heart, liver, kidneys, and gonads are packed into the front 15% of the body. A uniform olive brown, electric eels have only rudimentary gills that cannot sustain them underwater; they would drown if held down. Their only fins are small paired ones located behind the gills.

Electric eels have powerful electric organs that lie on either side of the vertebral column, extending almost the length of the fish and accounting for about 60% of its body weight. These organs have 5,000 to 6,000 electroplates, which are arranged like cells in a dry battery. These organs emit 2 kinds of discharges, one of high voltage (550 volts) for stunning prey and one that is much weaker, that it uses as a direction finder and an indicator for locating objects and prey in the vicinity. The latter use is crucial to its survival because these fish are blind at maturity. Strangely, electric eels do not try to kill their prey with an electric discharge but, rather, only to stun it. If a discharge kills the prey, the eel will not touch it.

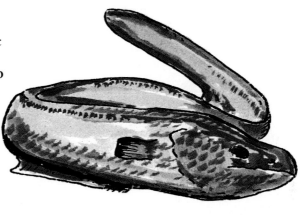

Eight hours after its death, an electric eel can still emit enough electricity to light up more than 200 neon bulbs.

Injury

The shock from an electric eel affects the body by altering physiological functions, such as involuntary muscle actions and respiration. Electric shock can also cause gangrene of muscle and other tissue, vertebral and other skeletal fractures, and torn muscles and tendons.

Symptoms

Symptoms may vary greatly depending on the magnitude of the current, body resistance, the pathway of the current through the body, and the duration of the current flow. A small shock may only startle a victim. More severe shocks can cause spastic stimulation and contraction of muscles, followed by hyperventilation, loss of reflex control, and unconsciousness. Both respiratory paralysis and cardiac failure may cause death.

Treatment

If the victim has stopped breathing, mouth-to-mouth resuscitation should be performed. In extreme cases a doctor may administer external cardiac massage. See Bites, Gorings, Maulings, and Shock, p. 112.

GARFISH

HOW IT GETS PEOPLE

Genera: Atractosteus and Lepisosteus

CLIMATIC ZONE

HOW IT GETS PEOPLE

HABITAT

RATING

CLIMATIC ZONE

General

Usually sluggish and idle but able to strike their prey quickly and efficiently, garfish are full of contradictions. These long–bodied predators can be found basking motionless near the surface of the water or lurking alongside submerged branches. In posture, form, and coloration they strongly resemble floating twigs and logs, for which they are often mistaken.

Garfish, also known as alligator gars, have irregular eating habits because of a very slow digestive system. But when they are hungry they can give chase very abruptly and are capable of literally bounding across the surface of the water in pursuit of aquatic birds or fish. Like crocodiles, they attack their prey with a broadside lunge and bite with long rows of sharp, needlelike teeth, which are designed for puncturing and holding prey.

Garfish

Their spearlike beak is very dangerous and can inflict serious internal injuries to humans. Graceful and swift in pursuit, gars have been known to leap out of the water (sometimes almost vertically) and impale fishers. The alligator gar has been called the "shark of fresh water."

Fossils of the two living genera of garfish have been recovered in archaeological digs in Europe, India, and North America and date back to the Tertiary and Cretaceous periods, some 70 million years ago. These ancient fish are characterized by their heavily armored scales, which do not overlap like normal fish scales, but are tightly articulated. These enameled scales are so hard and so strong that Native Americans used them as arrowheads and wore the skins as breastplates. The scales of older gars are tough enough to withstand a spear without being pierced. Today these armored scales are used to make costume jewelry in Mexico and the United States.

The eggs of two species of garfish have been reported to be toxic to humans. Among the myriad symptoms of this type of poisoning are swooning and a strange ringing in the ears.

Dangerous Water Creatures

Name/Description

Garfish belong to two genera, *Atractosteus* and *Lepisosteus*, and are long-bodied (about four feet long) predatory fish with spearlike snouts. Their extended jaws have very sharp, well-developed teeth, which they use to grasp and hold prey. Silvery, with blue or green backs, they have a very strong armor plating covering the pectoral area. Called a cuirass, it is composed of diamond-shaped scales that fit side by side instead of overlapping in the usual way. Their dorsal and anal fins are located in the posterior portion of their body. They detect their prey by sight and, when they are close, verify the location of their prey with the aid of sensory glands along their lateral sides. The garfish's swim bladder is connected to the esophagus and acts as a lung, enabling them to breathe atmospheric air.

Most garfish species migrate to coastal areas to spawn. Group spawning occurs from March to August, depending on the location, in shallow warm water and over vegetation. The adhesive eggs, about 27,000 per female, are scattered randomly and hatch within six to eight days. The baby gars cling to the vegetation by means of an adhesive pad on their snout.

Injury

The gar's long snout can cause puncture wounds. For symptoms, see Bites, Gorings, Maulings, and Shock, p. 112.

Toxicology

Two species of garfish may be ichthyotoxic (containing a poison exclusive to fish), with the poison usually restricted to its gonads. It has been established that there is a definite relationship between gonad activity and toxin production.

Symptoms

Symptoms develop soon after ingestion and include abdominal pain, nausea, vomiting, diarrhea, dizziness, headache, fever, bitter taste, dry-

Garfish

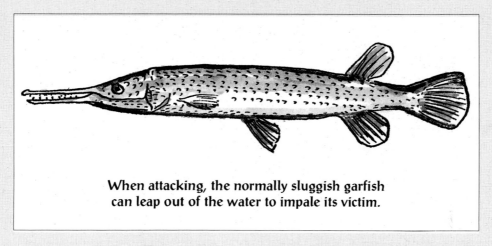

**When attacking, the normally sluggish garfish
can leap out of the water to impale its victim.**

ness of the mouth, intense thirst, a sensation of constriction in the chest, a rapid and irregular pulse, low blood pressure, cyanosis, dilated pupils, syncope (fainting, swooning), chills, dysphagia (difficulty in swallowing), and tinnitus (ringing in the ears). There have been no certified cases of acute or fatal garfish poisoning.

Treatment

A doctor may initiate gastric lavage (the washing out of the stomach or intestinal tract). There is no known antidote. The remainder of the treatment is symptomatic.

Prevention

• Eating the flesh and roe of garfish, especially during their reproduct-ive season, should be avoided.

• Although cooking is said to destroy most ichthyotoxins, one can never be sure.

HAWKSBILL TURTLE

HOW IT GETS PEOPLE

Eretmochelys imbricata

HABITAT

CLIMATIC ZONE

RATING

General

If a person, after a day in the hot tropical sun, eats a huge meal—perhaps including some exotic delicacies such as turtle meat—drinks some powerful rum punch, has halitosis (bad breath), and complains of nausea and cramps, it may be no serious problem at all. But if the person becomes sicker and cannot stay awake, he or she may be suffering from acute hawksbill turtle poisoning and may only have one chance in three of surviving. And even if the victim does survive, he or she may still have permanent liver or kidney damage.

Hawksbill turtles often feed on poisonous algae and, especially in the Caribbean, on poisonous sponges, which can render their flesh and liver extremely toxic. However, one's chances of being poisoned have greatly diminished, sadly enough, because this sea turtle is near extinction. Having overcome predators, climatic changes, and other hazards for 150 million years, hawksbill turtles have not been able to overcome the poacher's nets and have now completely disappeared from some tropical seas, with their numbers dwindling elsewhere. Although protected by law in many areas by law, the hawksbill turtle is still being poached in great quantities by impoverished tropical fishers unable to resist the tempting prices offered by illegal traders. In the Caribbean, one turtle can bring in more than a normal week's wages.

The turtles are hunted for their green skins, used in making leather; for hawksbill calipee, an edible, yellowish, jellylike substance that is the essential ingredient in turtle soup; and for their greatly prized tortoiseshells.

From colonial times until the 1930s, the Caribbean hawksbill was hunted avidly for its tortoiseshell, but the market declined dramatically with the introduction of synthetic imitations. In recent years, however, the market for genuine hawksbill products has grown, bolstered by Japanese consumers—reportedly the world's leading buyers of turtle products—and various trinket-buying tourists. In Costa Rica, the poaching is so extensive that whenever these turtles congregate at feeding reefs and rocks, the *careyeros'* (hawksbill fishers) boats gather in increasing numbers to harpoon them, in some cases coming by motorboat from as far as 50 miles away. Some fishers use the shark sucker (genus *Echeneis*)

to catch these turtles. These fish are equipped with a large suction plate on top of their head, with which they can firmly attach themselves to the turtle's plastron (central part of the shell). In Southeast Asia there is more control of hawksbill hunting because the people depend on hawksbill eggs as an important part of their essentially vegetarian diet. Nonetheless, poaching generally continues worldwide.

Name/Description

The hawksbill turtle (*Eretmochelys imbricata*) is an endangered carnivorous sea turtle with a flat, streamlined carapace (shell) that never completely becomes ossified (developed into bone). Even in old age, the ends of the hawksbill turtle's ribs are exposed. The carapace is covered with dark, mottled horny plates, overlapping toward the back like shingles. Broad, fat forelegs, like fins, serve for locomotion in water. Short hind legs act as rudders for steering. Only the female goes on land, to lay her eggs. She may bury up to 115 eggs on a beach, covering them with sand. She obliterates her tracks in and out of the water by throwing sand over her back with her front flippers as she moves along.

Hawksbill turtles eat fish, sponges, lower marine animals, and some algae and seaweed. They have very powerful jaws and usually weigh about 100 pounds. Even though they must breathe air, they can stay underwater for long periods of time.

Toxicology

The hawksbill turtle's toxic ingredient is chelotoxin (poison exclusively found in turtles) and is derived from the poisonous marine life on which they feed. See also Ciguatera Poisoning, p. 114.

Symptoms

Symptoms are nausea, vomiting, diarrhea, a burning sensation of the lips, tongue, and mouth, tightening of the chest, cramps, difficulty in

There is no known antidote for hawksbill turtle poisoning.

swallowing, hypersalivation, foul breath, skin rash, sloughing of the skin, and enlargement of the liver. If poisoning is severe, lethargy sets in. The worst sign is a victim becoming so sleepy that it is hard to keep him or her awake. In extreme cases, coma precedes death.

Treatment

There is no known antidote, and the fatality rate for victims of hawksbill turtle poisoning ranges from 28% to 44%. See Ciguatera Poisoning, p. 114.

Prevention

• Refrain from eating turtle liver, meat, or eggs.

MORAY EEL

HOW IT GETS PEOPLE

Genus: Muraena

HABITAT

HOW IT GETS PEOPLE

CLIMATIC ZONE

CLIMATIC ZONE

RATING

General

Slithering through almost all tropical seas, moray eels are a perfect example of nature's version of double jeopardy: a victim can die from being bitten by or from biting into this violently toxic fish.

The moray gets its scientific name from Licinius Murdena, a powerful Roman who lived toward the end of the second century B.C. and who kept these ugly predators in special breeding tanks, called *vivaria*, as a demonstration of his wealth. Another Roman, Vedius Pollo, entertained his dinner guests by letting them watch his pet morays eat disobedient slaves. According to the ancient Roman chronicler Pliny the Elder, threats of a fatal trip to these tanks kept slaves in line.

Notoriously powerful biters, their curved teeth are quite terrifying and highly visible as they open and close their mouths to breathe. Moray teeth were unearthed in a Pleistocene deposit dating back two million years. Nocturnal, moray eels spend the day hiding in the cracks and crevices of rocky coasts and coral reefs. In the evenings, they begin their quest for food, feeding mostly on fish, shrimp, other crustaceans, and sometimes on the fingertips of an unwary diver. "Fingers look like food," says moray expert Dee Scarr, who in her hundreds of interactions with moray eels in the Dutch Antilles has never once been bitten. Her secret is the brightly colored gloves she wears. Moray eels are less likely to attack because they do not eat brightly colored food. Said to be nonaggressive, morays usually bite (with a grip described as "deep, crushing, and tenacious") when a foot or hand is inadvertently placed in their lair. They strike with great rapidity, and according to Dr. Bruce Halstead, one of the pioneers in the study of dangerous marine life, "they maintain their bulldog–like grip until death."

In spite of their snakelike appearance and repulsive skin (their leathery skin has mucous glands that make them shiny and extremely slippery), moray eels are still highly prized. One species in particular, *Muraena helena*, is still found in Mediterranean fish markets. It is said that the Roman emperor Julius Caesar served up 6,000 of them at a banquet. No matter how tasty moray eels may be, eating them can be a fatal mistake because they can be violently toxic and may produce painful convulsions before a speedy death.

Dangerous Water Creatures

Name/Description
Moray eels, of the genus *Muraena*, are often brightly colored eels of the family Muraenidae. They comprise about 40 species worldwide.

Their sharp pointed teeth are capable of inflicting a savage bite. Their body is very muscular and is compressed laterally; the tough skin is leathery and lacks scales. Size varies from species to species—the gray moray (*Gymnothorax griseus*) of the Red Sea is only about 20 inches long, whereas the Indo-Pacific moray eel (*Thrsoidea macrurus*) has been measured at more than 10 feet. They can live for up to 27 years.

Injury
The moray eel's very powerful jaws and sharp teeth can inflict severe lacerations; wounds are jagged and torn and can readily become infected.

Toxicology
The moray's principal toxin is ciguatoxin, which is a potent nerve poison that remains unaffected if the fish is cooked or frozen. Moray eel intoxications are often more severe than other ciguatoxications (see Ciguatera Poisoning, p. 114) because moray eels have proportionately higher concentrations of poison than do other toxic fish.

Symptoms
Injury: Wounds can easily develop secondary infections. If there is an acute blood loss, the victim could go into shock and die.

Ingestion: Symptoms, which may develop within 20 minutes, include tingling around the lips, tongue, and throat before spreading to the hands and feet, accompanied by heaviness in the legs. This tingling may be followed by numbness, nausea, vomiting, abdominal cramps, diarrhea, a metallic taste, throat spasms, excessive mucous production, foaming at the mouth, muscular weakness, perspiration, high temperature, visual impairment, skin rash, crying out in pain, paralysis of the respiratory muscles, and general lack of motor coordination. These symptoms may lead to violent convulsions, coma, and death.

Moray Eel

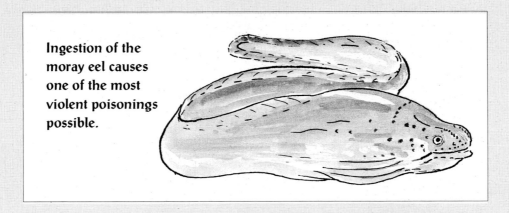

Ingestion of the moray eel causes one of the most violent poisonings possible.

Treatment

Injury: Treatment is much the same as for a barracuda bite. Immediately try to control the blood loss. Use a compression bandage if the wound is oozing. Antibiotics may be administered by a doctor to prevent infection.

Ingestion: Treatment of ciguatoxins is largely symptomatic. There are no known specific antidotes. The stomach should be emptied by gastric lavage, emetics (agents that induce vomiting), or saline purges. Some severe cases have responded well to intravenously administered 10% calcium gluconate. The acute symptoms usually subside within 10 days in the milder form, although in some, symptoms have lingered for up to two months.

Prevention

• Once the teeth are imbedded in the flesh, experts recommend that victims of a moray eel bite "grin and bear it" until the eel realizes it is not eating a fish and lets go.

• If bitten, do not try to grab the eel with your free hand or it may attack that; one experienced diver tried this tactic and ended up with wounds on both hands requiring 27 stitches.

• Be careful around coral reefs and submerged wreckage.

OCTOPUS

HOW IT GETS PEOPLE

Genus: Octopus

HABITAT

CLIMATIC ZONE

CLIMATIC ZONE

RATING

General

When asked quickly to name a creature the feet or arms of which are directly attached to its head, most people just look baffled. But that is exactly the characteristic that makes the octopus a member of the cephalopod group of mollusks. Resembling a creature from a science fiction movie, the octopus has long been the subject of folklore, myth, and literature. For example, American writer John Steinbeck, in his novel *Cannery Row*, called it a "creeping murderer" that "oozes and flows."

This denizen of the deep has been wrongfully accused of many acts, but it is far from harmless and will even come ashore in search of prey (usually shore–dwelling rats). In 1917 a parson was taking a group of boys on an outing along the Victoria coast of Australia when an octopus left the water and attacked, rapidly encircling the parson with its arms. A good–sized beast, it took the combined efforts of several of the parson's young charges to disentangle him. However, if he had been swimming, the parson might not have been so lucky. Already at a considerable disadvantage underwater, a human would be particularly

Octopus

vulnerable if attacked near a solid anchor point, which the octopus could grasp with one of its long arms. In *Kingdom of the Octopus*, Frank Lane made the following calculations: a 200-pound inert man can be held underwater by a pull of about 10 pounds; a medium-sized octopus can greatly exceed that pull. So even a strongly resisting victim, tightly held by an octopus anchored firmly to a solid foundation, would drown. Usually shy and afraid of humans, it is believed that an octopus will never attack unless provoked, for example, by a diver inadvertently intruding into an underwater cave lair or when a sexually excited octopus mistakes a human arm or leg for a potential mate.

Not only can octopuses attack by grabbing with their arms and drowning their victims; they can also bite, leaving two, often deep, puncture wounds. Octopuses are capable of envenomization—their posterior salivary glands secrete a poison that they use to stun and kill their prey. But only the blue-ringed octopus has proved fatal to humans.

Octopuses, among the most active and elaborately constructed mollusks, are surprisingly clever creatures. They can move quickly through the sea, clouding the surrounding water with their ink. The ink confuses potential predators into thinking that the ink cloud is actually the

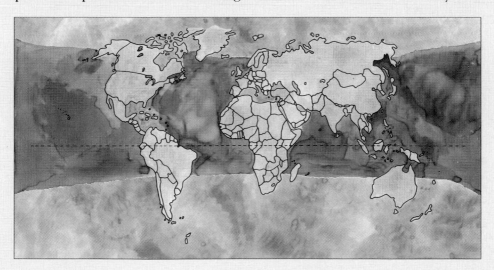

octopus or some other quarry. Able to hang suspended in the water, they can patiently lie in wait for hours for prey to pass. Octopuses are also capable of changing color to a degree and with a speed that rivals that of the chameleon.

Name/Description

Octopuses comprise about 150 species of a single genus belonging to the cephalopod class of mollusks. The word *octopus* comes from Greek and can be loosely translated as "eight-footed." Octopuses have a highly concentrated central nervous system protected by a cartilaginous (composed of cartilage) cranium, and they have image-forming eyes much like those of vertebrates. These carnivorous predators are active hunting animals and defend their established territories. Their saclike bodies have no fins or skeleton and vary in size from the two-inch *Octopus arborescens* to the gargantuan *O. apollyon*—one specimen measured 23 feet from arm tip to arm tip and weighed more than 118 pounds. Ninety-six percent of the octopus's body length is made up of its long arms. On the inner surface of the eight arms are suckers, adjustable disks consisting of a muscular membrane with a thick rim, which can be controlled by the octopus with delicate precision. Although octopuses frequently crawl across the sea floor with their arms, they usually move, often with incredible speed, by jetting water from an adjustable siphon, and they can squeeze through any hole large enough to admit their hard, parrot-like beak.

Octopuses reproduce sexually, meaning that they reproduce through the union of males and females. The function of the penis is performed by one of the male's arms, known as the hectocotylus, which conveys packets of spermatozoa into the female cavity. At copulation this arm becomes detached and remains there. The female's nidamental glands produce protective capsules around yolky eggs from which the young octopuses hatch. The female unfortunately spends so much time attending to the masses of eggs that she neglects her own well-being and dies soon after her young begin hatching.

Octopus

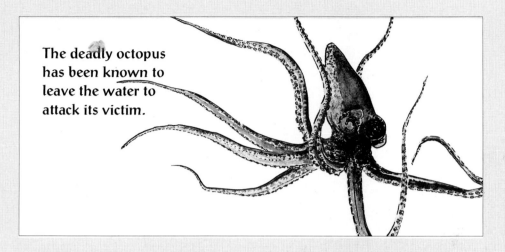

The deadly octopus has been known to leave the water to attack its victim.

Toxicology

The posterior salivary glands of the octopus secrete a cephalotoxin (poison found in cephalopods), a glycoprotein of immense complexity that has a paralyzing action on crustaceans, apparently inhibiting respiration. This toxin can also affect humans.

Symptoms

In victims of octopus bites, there will be a local burning sensation around the site of the puncture wounds. Even if there is no envenomization, these wounds are subject to secondary infection. Profuse bleeding has been reported in some cases, which may indicate that there is an anticoagulant constituent in the venom. Usually, a victim experiences only local and temporary discomfort.

Treatment

Wounds should be cleaned with an antiseptic. A doctor may prescribe an analgesic for pain.

Prevention

• Be cautious in the vicinity of underwater caves.

PIRANHA

HOW IT GETS PEOPLE

Genera: Serrasalmus, Pygocetrus, Pygopristis

HABITAT

CLIMATIC ZONE

RATING

General

Probably the first reliable studies of the piranha were made in 1799 by Alexander von Humboldt and Aime Bonpland on their 1,700-mile journey up South America's Orinoco River. The German baron described the piranha as a "fish only a foot long with teeth so sharp and jaws so strong it can chop out a piece of flesh from a man or an alligator as neatly as a razor, or clip off a finger or toe, bone and all, with the dispatch of a meat cleaver." And when the travelogue *Through the Brazilian Wilderness*, by Theodore Roosevelt, first appeared, its sensationalistic descriptions of the "most ferocious fish in the world" made it the "darling" of jungle writers. Roosevelt describes the tenacious fish: "They will snap a finger off a hand incautiously trailed in the water; they mutilate swimmers—in every town in Paraguay they devour alive any wounded man or beast; for blood in the water excites them to madness."

58

Piranha

The late William T. Innes, an authority on home aquariums, described a movie taken of an attack. A young pig was dipped into a Brazilian stream several times, and as Innes reports, "each time it was lifted out of the water, it was reduced in size." After only two minutes, all that was left of the swine was the skeleton. In 1963, when Nicholas Guppy visited Apoera on the Courantyne River in Guyana, he found that most of the adult population there had lost fingers, toes, or penny-sized chunks of their arms or legs after bathing or washing clothes. One boy at nearby Orealla had most of his foot bitten off and spent months in the hospital. In September 1981 more than 300 people were reputedly killed and eaten when an overloaded passenger–cargo boat capsized and sank as it was docking at the Brazilian port of Obidos. As Dr. James Atz said of the South American piranha, "It is prevalent enough to make swimming or wading an extremely risky pastime over about half an entire continent."

Until recently, piranhas were imported into many countries alive for home aquarists. Extremely expensive, the piranha's high price was the result of a shipping problem. A can that normally would be used to ship

100 smaller fish had to be used for a single piranha. It seems that the voracious piranhas are not above making meals out of their fellow piranhas. Today there are widespread injunctions against the sale of the fish, perhaps from the fear of their escape and establishment in local waterways. Also, many former piranha enthusiasts now favor other species. Perhaps they learned from the story of the man who, without thinking, scooped up his escaped piranha with his bare hands. The fish slashed his fingers before he could drop it back into the water.

Name/Description

Piranhas are small characin fish (a large group of strong–jawed fresh–water fish), 14 to 28 inches long, that inhabit the wide, sluggish rivers of South America. Their jaws are short, broad, and so powerful that they can bite off a person's finger or toe as if it were a carrot. They have one row of triangular teeth, which snap together in a razor–sharp bite. The three genera of piranhas, of the family Characidae, are *Serrasalmus*, *Pygocetrus*, and *Pygopristis*. *Serrasalmus natteri* is probably the most lethal species of these predatory fish.

Injury

Although piranhas can bite off only a thimbleful of flesh at one time, they attack in schools of up to 1,000. Thus, even a large animal, such as a cow or a human, can be eaten in minutes. There is record of a 100–pound capybara (the largest extant rodent; a tailless, partially web-footed animal found in South American rivers) being reduced to a skeleton in less than one minute. A wounded alligator was stripped of all flesh in five minutes.

Treatment

See Bites, Gorings, Maulings, and Shock, p. 112.

Piranhas can reduce a pig to bones in less than two minutes and can do the same to an alligator in less than five.

Prevention

• Never bathe, wade, swim, wash clothes, or even test the temperature of the water in the sluggish rivers of South America.

PORTUGUESE MAN-OF-WAR

Physalia physalis and Physalia utriculus

HOW IT GETS PEOPLE

CLIMATIC ZONE

RATING

HABITAT

General

When a young American serviceman was admitted to the U.S. Naval Dispensary in Puerto Rico, his condition was described as being "as though he was recovering from an epileptic convulsion . . . eyes staring widely, incoherent, breathing with such difficulty that each outgoing breath came as a cough. Across his back and left shoulder was an angry, red rash and the skin on the rest of his body was flushed." In the Philippines, when the dead body of a 19–year–old man was examined, "no wound was found . . . except a purplish livid discoloration practically encircling the right leg and knees." The "angry, red rash" and "purplish livid discoloration" both had been caused by one of the most dangerous organisms known, the Portuguese man–of–war. Its sting is said to be so excruciatingly painful that native pearl and sponge divers dread it more than they dread even the most vicious of sharks. Even after it has been dead and laid out on the beach for several days, its tentacles are still capable of inflicting severe stings.

Portuguese Man-of-War

Likened to an "untidy jellyfish," the Portuguese man-of-war acts like a single entity but is actually a symbiotic (close union of dissimilar organisms) colony composed of four different organisms: a balloon-like pneumatophore, which keeps the colony together and afloat, and which contains a toxic gas that can harm the eyes if punctured; gastrozooids, which are feeding polyps that gather food; dactylozooids, or tentacle polyps, which contain the nematocysts; and the gonozooids, which enable the colony to reproduce. The colony, with almost 1,000 individual organisms, behaves like a predatory animal, inflicting stings that have been compared to "being struck by a bolt of lightning."

Thomas Helm, who has written about dangerous marine animals, relates his experience of being stung by a Portuguese man-of-war: "In some respects my contact with the Portuguese man-of-war was comparable to an electric jolt, except that it grew more intense as I hastily withdrew. Sensing that I had acted unwisely, I began swimming rapidly toward the beach. Although I was in excellent physical condition and a better than average swimmer, I discovered I was rapidly losing muscular

control and I began to wonder if I was going to maintain sufficient coordination long enough to keep from drowning."

In spite of its killer instinct, the Portuguese man–of–war protects other creatures, such as the bluebottle fish (*Nomeus gronovii*), which it allows to swim amid its tentacles in search of its own prey. The Portuguese man–of–war has no control over its own destiny, resting almost helplessly upon the surface of tropical seas worldwide. Its pneumatophore, which floats above the surface of the water, acts as a sail and responds to changes in temperature and wind, directing the organism to milder environments.

Name/Description
The Portuguese man–of–war is a large free-swimming hydroid (a form of coelenterate that is asexual and grows into branching colonies by budding). It has a large sac (one foot long) with a broad crest on the upper side, from which the colony hangs as it floats on the surface of the sea. Its trailing bluish filaments are composed of medusas (the reproductive form) and polyps (the feeding form). The strands are made up of other types of polyps armed with numerous nematocysts, each containing a coiled venomous "harpoon" that is discharged on touch. Each tentacle may contain three quarters of a million nematocysts. They travel in tremendously long lines and schools. There are two species: the larger Atlantic species (*Physalia physalis*), found in the tropical Atlantic, West Indies, Mediterranean, and as far north as Scotland; and the smaller Indo–Pacific species (*Physalia utriculus*), which is found in Hawaii, Japan, and throughout the Indo–Pacific region.

Toxicology
The toxic principles of a Portuguese man–of–war's venom are tetramine and 5-hydroxytryamine. One large Portuguese man–of–war can easily kill an adult.

Symptoms
Even with mild envenomization, some swimmers go into shock and drown. Most victims experience immediate and intense stinging, throb-

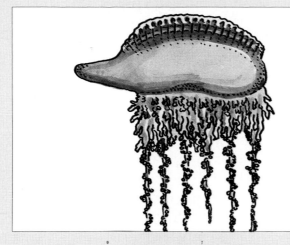

Victims compare the sting of the Portuguese man-of-war to a bolt of lightning.

bing, and burning pain that can last for hours. Purple swollen wheals may appear, along with blistering of the skin. These symptoms are followed by muscle spasms with violent shivering, difficulty in breathing, cardiac weakness, anxiety, profuse sweating, and swelling of the affected extremity. With severe envenomization, the victim may go into shock or a coma or may even die.

Treatment
Generously apply vinegar, lemon juice, sodium bicarbonate, or diluted acetic acid to deactivate the stinging nematocysts. Dust the affected area with flour or baking powder, then carefully scrape off the powder and its adhering nematocysts. With sterile tweezers, carefully remove any remaining fragments from the victim. Topical anti–inflammatory cortisone should reduce swelling. In cases of shock and respiratory distress, epinephrine may be administered intravenously by a doctor, as well as meperidine for pain and 10% calcium gluconate for muscle spasm. (See Bites, Gorings, Maulings, and Shock, p. 112.)

Prevention
• Be on guard for Portuguese men–of–war during their active season, December through April.

PUFFER FISH

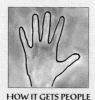

HOW IT GETS PEOPLE

Spheroides testudineus

HABITAT

HOW IT GETS PEOPLE

CLIMATIC ZONE

RATING

HABITAT

General

In Japan, tourists who sample a taste of fugu, which has been described as the "ultimate aesthetic experience," may later wish they had refrained. This extremely dangerous stew contains the highly toxic puffer fish. Its poison is 500 times stronger than cyanide. Although cooks who prepare fugu and chiri (another puffer dish) are required to attend a special school and receive a degree in puffer preparation, as many as 90 people are poisoned annually, with a 60% mortality rate. Amazingly enough, when eaten as sashimi (sliced raw), this leathery, coarse, scaleless fish is relatively safe. However, the Japanese prefer it cooked for its exhilarating physiological aftereffects: a mild numbing and tingling of the tongue and lips, a sensation of warmth, a flushing of the skin, and a general feeling of euphoria, placing it on a fine line between food and drug.

Puffer Fish

The strange effects of puffer poisonings were studied by Wade Davis, an ethnobiologist at Harvard University. He discovered puffer poison to be an essential ingredient in occult zombie potions. Although quite skeptical about zombiism, Davis noted similarities between the supposed zombies and the victims of puffer poisoning. In both cases, the body's vital signs can become so faint that the victim appears dead. In one instance, Japanese doctors believed a chiri peddler to be dead, only to have him walk out of the hospital 14 hours later. In another case, a man who "died" from eating fugu woke up seven days later in the morgue. Even eerier, in July 1984 a man revived after being nailed into his own coffin. Perhaps the worst aspect of puffer poisoning is that the victim remains totally aware and acutely alert—even though seemingly dead—until the moment of actual death, meaning that the fugu victim was quite aware of the lid being nailed down on his own coffin. It is now customary in Japan to leave the corpse of a puffer victim alongside his coffin for several days before burial.

In 1989 the U.S. Food and Drug Administration finally permitted the importation of puffer fish but subjected them to far more vigorous

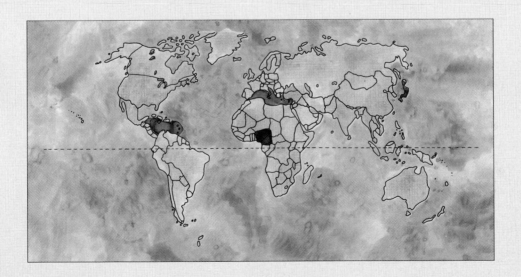

controls and inspections than any other seafood in the United States. Now, in New York, a plate of fugu hors d'oeuvres costs about $60.

Name/Description

Puffer fish (*Spheroides testudineus*) are members of the globefish (Tetradon-toidae) family. The common names of puffer and blowfish refer to their defense mechanism: When threatened they inflate an intestinal sac, blowing themselves into a globular shape, making it more difficult for predators to swallow them. In this state they float belly–up, eyes protruded, fins extended, incapable of generating motion. Puffers are equipped with powerful jaw muscles and teeth fused into plates, well suited for biting crabs, snails, mussels, and coral. They shoot out streams of water to stir up prey on the sea floor.

Toxicology

The chief component of puffer poison is the lethal neurotoxin tetro-dotoxin, which is stored in the gonads, especially the ovaries. It is also found in the puffer fish's roe, skin, liver, and intestines. Approximately 8 to 10 milligrams of this toxin is fatal. The fish is most toxic during its reproductive cycle and therefore should be avoided especially from May to July.

Symptoms

Symptoms vary with the amount ingested but start with malaise, pallor, dizziness, tingling of the lips and tongue, and ataxia (confusion). There will be numbness, hypersalivation, profuse sweating, extreme weakness, headache, subnormal temperature, decreased blood pressure, and a rapid, weak pulse. There may be nausea, vomiting, and diarrhea. Pupils become constricted, then dilated. Initial muscular twitching terminates in extensive paralysis. Victims may become comatose but in most cases

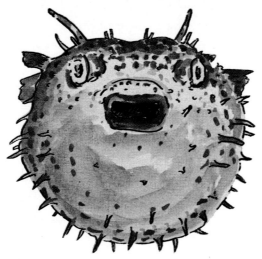

**A single lethal dose of puffer fish toxin
can fit on the head of a pin.**

retain consciousness. Mental faculties remain acute until shortly before death, which is caused mainly by respiratory paralysis.

Treatment

There is no known antidote, and poisoning can be treated only symptomatically. Induced vomiting at a very early stage has proved helpful. A doctor might conduct artificial respiration or cardiac massage if those treatments are deemed necessary. There are no latent effects of the toxin—should one survive puffer fish poisoning.

Prevention

• Do not eat fugu, chiri, or any other dish containing this toxic creature.

SCORPIONFISH

HOW IT GETS PEOPLE

Genus: Scorpaena

HABITAT

CLIMATIC ZONE

CLIMATIC ZONE

RATING

General

Like a well–camouflaged guerrilla warrior, the dangerous but eerily beautiful scorpionfish motionlessly stands guard over its coral reef beneath the sea. Confident of its highly developed defense system (a series of venomous spines that poison on contact), it will neither attack an innocent swimmer nor move away when one approaches. Able to remain motionless for so long that algae will grow on it, the scorpionfish (and the closely related stonefish) can, like a chameleon, change its color to match the background, making it all but invisible to divers. And many divers who have survived envenomization by these deadly fish have lived to tell of a pain that made them shoot straight out of the sea upon contact.

Dr. M. Findlay–Russell, an expert on toxins and director of neurological research at Loma Linda University, writes, "I have injected small doses of a number of different venoms into myself and have found none quite as painful as those of the stingray and [scorpionfish]." Not only is

70

there intense pain and "rather remarkable swelling" (legs may attain elephantine proportions), but there is also lasting stiffness and loss of sensitivity in the area around the sting.

Dr. J. L. B. Smith, a marine biologist who was accidentally stabbed by a stonefish in the tidal shallows off the coast of Portuguese East Africa in the 1950s, describes the pain as being "of an intensity never before experienced" by him. A full day after the envenomization, he noted the ongoing effects: "Twenty-four hours after the stab, large yellow blisters started to form and spread rapidly over the thumb, becoming extremely painful, and when punctured released a serous fluid, which dripped steadily thereafter for six days." Dr. Smith suffered from the intoxication for more than two months, commenting, "After eighty days, the hand was still weak and the thumb barely movable at the joints, being still slightly swollen and painful when moved. The toxin had a marked adverse effect on my general health and condition."

Despite the dangers of the scorpionfish, many fishers brave catching them because of their high commercial value—their meat is said to be quite tender and tasty. Surprisingly enough, there is no danger in eating the fish, only in touching it.

Fortunately, the acute pain of a scorpionfish sting can be relieved if treated with hot water. Scorpionfish venom, like that of the stingray, is heat labile (sensitive to changes in temperature) and is quickly broken down when heated. Rapid immersion in very hot water will usually ease a good part of the pain. Some savvy divers now even carry thermoses of hot water with them for just such a purpose if they know they might come across a scorpionfish.

Name/Description

Scorpionfish comprise numerous species of the genus *Scorpaena* and the family Scorpaenidae, which also includes zebra fish (*Pterois*) and stonefish (*Synanceja*). Their outer skin and bone structure is covered with horny, spiky, scaly appendages. Poison glands are located at the base of their fins. When the fish is agitated it erects its dorsal fin, flares its other fins, and thrashes about. Ranging from 12 to 18 inches long, scorpionfish have a large vacuum–cleaner–like mouth that inhales prey such as small shellfish and shrimp. They are especially dangerous because of their excellent camouflage; they can vary their color to match the background, and because of their ability to remain motionless for a long time they blend in quite effectively with the rubble- and algae-covered coral and outcroppings on the ocean floor.

Toxicology

Scorpionfish venom is neurotoxic, which means that it affects the central nervous system, and it is hemotoxic, which means that it affects the red blood cells as well. Whereas most victims are envenomed by stepping on one, some others are poisoned by touch. In some species the venom is as toxic as that of the cobra and remains potent in the fish's body for as long as 48 hours after it has died.

Symptoms

Symptoms vary greatly according to the location of the envenomization, the severity of the poisoning, the victim's age, and possible allergies to

Scorpionfish

If poisoned by a scorpionfish, a victim's limbs can swell to elephantine proportions.

the venom. Generally, there is immediate and intensely throbbing pain, often causing the victim to scream and thrash about on the ground. (Dr. Smith talks about an "insane desire to ease the mounting agony by rolling around on the floor.") This pain is followed by redness, swelling, perspiration, pallor, restlessness, nausea, vomiting, and diarrhea. More serious effects are delirium, convulsions, prostration, respiratory distress, and cardiac failure. Some victims have died within six hours of being envenomed. In nonfatal stingings, secondary bacterial infections, tetanus, and primary shock are frequent complications.

Treatment

The area affected with scorpionfish venom should be immersed in very hot water—but not above 120 degrees Fahrenheit—for about an hour. The venom will be neutralized quickly by the heat. The victim should be given plenty of fluids, because excessive perspiration will lead to dehydration. A doctor may inject a local anesthetic to relieve pain. See also, Bites, Gorings, Maulings, and Shock, p. 112.

Prevention

• Wear protective footwear when wading in scorpionfish–infested waters.

• Skin divers should be especially cautious.

• Be careful on or around coral reefs.

SEA CUCUMBER

HOW IT GETS PEOPLE

Class: Holothurioidea

HABITAT

HOW IT GETS PEOPLE

CLIMATIC ZONE

RATING

General

There is nothing very exciting about cucumbers—not their shape, color, consistency, or taste. Nevertheless, they are said to be "cool." Among their many other uses, women rub their faces with cucumber slices, using them as a refreshing astringent. More often, cucumbers are employed as food, such as cold cucumber soup, a delight on a hot summer's day. And fresh cucumber juice is an essential ingredient in a good gazpacho (a cold Spanish soup). Before partaking of any of these culinary delights, one should be sure that the cucumber was harvested from the garden and not the sea—because sea cucumbers, which are actually a type of animal, can inflict a fatal poisoning.

For ages, South Sea Islanders have placed toxic sea cucumber juice in water to kill or stupefy fish. (The fish die quickly from complete muscular paralysis.) The Chinese consider sea cucumbers, which they call sea slugs, items of haute cuisine. In the Indo–Pacific, where sea cucumbers are also known as bechê–de–mer and trepang, they are used to flavor

Sea Cucumber

soups and stews—after first being boiled so that the sea cucumbers will eviscerate (purge their own internal organs), shorten, and thicken.

Knowing that many species of sea cucumbers are toxic should make one consider staying away from them, but knowing that they eviscerate themselves should remove all doubt. These sluglike creatures of the deep can, under hostile conditions, disembowel themselves by forcing their visceral (vital internal) organs out through their anus. A person would literally have to be "cool as a cucumber" to witness this primitive self-defense process without becoming sick to his or her own stomach.

Usually found on the ocean floor, where they camouflage and hide under rocks and coral, very little is known about sea cucumbers, though knowledge of their toxicity has existed for more than a century. It is known, however, that 24 out of 27 of the sea cucumber species from the Indo-Pacific region are poisonous—a high enough percentage to make anyone wary.

Name/Description

Sea cucumbers are any of a group of echinoderms (sea cucumbers belong to the phylum Echinodermata, which also includes starfish and

sea urchins) of the class Holothurioidea. They have a sausage- or cucumber-shaped body with leathery, often warty skin and have 10 or more branched tentacles around the mouth, which is located at the anterior end of the body. Usually a dark, dull color, these marine invertebrates usually live for three years and vary greatly in length—the smallest, at 1/7 of an inch long, is *Psammothuria ganapatii*; the longest are members of the genus *Synapta*, which can stretch up to 40 inches long. The intestinal tract of a sea cucumber is long and looped and terminates in an anus at the posterior end. The anus is used for both respiration and discharge.

Sea cucumbers have what are called organs of cuvier, which consists of pink, red, or white tubules attached to the common stem of the respiratory "trees." When a sea cucumber is irritated, these organs swell and elongate into slender, sticky threads that serve to entangle a predator. In some species these organs contain a large concentration of toxin.

Locomotion is achieved by means of rhythmic contractions of the body along the sea floor. Most species of sea cucumbers have five rows of tube feet extending from the mouth to the anus, but these extensions are used primarily for attachment.

Sea cucumbers are ancient creatures; their fossil spicules (pointed, fleshy superficial appendages) have been discovered in rocks of Ordovician age (the fourth period of the Paleozoic era)—some 500 million years ago.

Toxicology

Sea cucumbers possess small skin glands that excrete venom. The more important source of envenomization, however, are the organs of cuvier. When a sea cucumber is endangered, the cuvier's tubules are ejected from the body cavity through the anus and upon contacting water swell and elongate into sticky threads. There is no difference between the holothurinotoxins (poisons found in sea cucumbers) from the skin and those from the organs of cuvier.

Sea Cucumber

The sea cucumber can disembowel itself and regenerate new internal organs in less than a month.

Symptoms

Ingestion: Ingestion of toxic sea cucumbers can lead to severe and sometimes fatal intoxication. But human poisonings have been so rare and remote that there are few reliable records of symptoms. In mild cases digestive problems result. Extreme cases have caused paralysis and death.

Touch: There will be burning pain, redness, and a violent inflammatory reaction. If the toxic fluid gets in the eye, it can cause blindness.

Treatment

Ingestion: Treatment is symptomatic. Anticholinesterase agents may be effective.

Touch: Symptoms usually disappear spontaneously. Treatment is symptomatic, if needed at all.

Prevention

- It is wise to refrain from dishes in the Indo–Pacific region that are seasoned with trepang.

- Gloves should be worn when handling sea cucumbers.

SEA SNAKE

HOW IT GETS PEOPLE

Family: Hydrophiidae

HABITAT

CLIMATIC ZONE

RATING

General

There are certain places one expects to encounter snakes: in the shade of boulders in the western desert; slithering through the weeds beside a lake; sometimes even curled up in the sleeping bag of an unsuspecting camper. The last place one would think to encounter a snake would be in the sea, but that is exactly where some of the most dangerous snakes in the world reside.

The dangers of certain sea creatures, such as sharks, stonefish, bar–racuda, and even sea urchins, are well known. But the number of people who even know about the existence of sea snakes is unbelievably small. Not only do sea snakes exist, but they can be found in every ocean of the world except the Atlantic. Sea snakes are often mistaken for some kind of eel, but they are real snakes. They belong to the elapid family and are closely related to cobras, mambas, kraits, and coral snakes but have an even more deadly neurotoxin. Like land snakes, sea snakes breathe air, but because of adaptations better suited to a marine en–vironment—broad scales on the stomach and a vertically compressed body—they are rather helpless on land. All sea snakes have fixed fangs,

78

Sea Snake

rather than the retractable fangs of most venomous land snakes. For this reason, they attack with a deliberate bite rather than with a quick strike.

One of the problems with the sea snake is that its bite is painless and its venom is slow acting, so that by the time symptoms develop, it may be too late for medical aid. This lack of pain and immediate symptoms may make victims and those around them doubt that there was a bite at all. An incident that happened a number of years ago in Malaya illustrates this problem quite vividly. An 8-year-old boy was wading in shallow water 10 feet from shore. He looked down and saw a snake fastened to his ankle. There was no pain, but when the snake released its grip, the frightened boy showed the bite marks to his father. The father dismissed the marks and let the boy go back into the water to play. Within an hour the boy began to feel stiffness and muscle weakness. Four hours after being bitten he became drowsy. At midnight there was blood in his urine. At that point his father, who appears to have been somewhat nonchalant about the whole thing, called a doctor. In another four hours the boy's breathing became rapid and rather noisy, and he was finally taken to a hospital. The doctor at the hospital suspected polio, which seems to indicate that the father had neglected

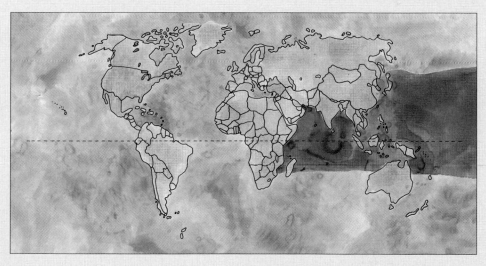

to even tell him about the snake. The little boy's condition continued to deteriorate until he died, 13 hours after being bitten. This long period between envenomization and death is not unusual, and even longer periods of time have elapsed between bite and death. Another incident involves a 54-year-old fisherman who was admitted to a hospital eight days after being bitten by a sea snake; he died four days later, 12 days after the bite.

Name/Description

Sea snakes are any of numerous venomous aquatic snakes of warm seas, comprising about 50 species of 2 subfamilies of Hydrophiidae. The most venomous is the *Hydrophis belcheri*, which has venom 100 times more toxic than the Australian taipan. Air breathers, their nostrils are on top of their snout and have watertight, valvelike closures. Superb swimmers, they have flattened, oarlike tails and can move backward and forward in water with equal rapidity. Although sea snakes average four to six feet in length, some species can reach up to nine feet. The head of a sea snake is very small, perhaps developed to enter the burrows of the small eels upon which they feed. Sea snakes have a special gland that desalinates water and, in some species, a long, specialized lung that allows them to stay underwater for two to three hours. Their metabolism is very slow, and their fangs are permanently erect, front fixed, hollow, and not very large. The venom glands are located just below the eyes. Sea snakes are mostly found in shallow water, often floating on or near the surface.

Toxicology

Sea snake venom is not very well understood, but it contains an anticoagulant and a very potent neurotoxin that causes paralysis. The venom is unusual in that it has a direct effect on muscles.

All sea snakes possess in their venom glands many times the amount lethal to humans. When a sea snake bites, it releases all of its venom, and it takes several days for the venom to be regenerated. Thus, the degree of envenomization in a subsequent bite depends on the amount of venom available in the glands.

Sea snakes are found in every ocean in the world except the Atlantic.

Symptoms

Symptoms vary greatly because the amount of venom can range from none at all to as much as a lethal dose. At first, except for perhaps the feeling of a pin prick, there are no symptoms. Some victims have reported a sense of formication (a sensation that feels like ants crawling over one's skin). With very minor envenomization there may be some muscle pain, which usually goes away in one to three days.

Symptoms of more serious envenomization in addition to muscle pain are a thick feeling in the tongue, thirst, sweating, vomiting, and headache. Movement of the limbs is difficult and painful. There may be lockjaw; ptosis (drooping of the eyelids), an early and important sign of sea snake envenomization that is often mistaken for drowsiness; and finally, complete paralysis. Death will result from either respiratory failure, cardiac arrest, or renal (kidney) failure. It can occur anywhere from 3 to 24 hours after the bite.

Treatment

An antivenin for sea snake bites is available, and it should be administered immediately. Recovery is usually rapid after antivenin treatment. Supplementary treatment may include transfusions, tetanus injections, and antibiotics.

Prevention

• The *U.S. Navy Amphibious Forces Manual* offers the best advice with respect to sea snakes: Avoid them.

SEA URCHIN

Phylum: Echinodermata

HOW IT GETS PEOPLE

HABITAT

HABITAT

RATING

HOW IT GETS PEOPLE

HOW IT GETS YOU

CLIMATIC ZONE

CLIMATIC ZONE

General

All urchins are reputed to be naughty and mischievous, but any urchin that can burrow through steel is downright terrifying. With its incredibly strong spines, the sea urchin Strongylocentrotus has been known to burrow through steel three–fourths of an inch thick. On the coast of California in the 1920s, piers were built with steel piles instead of with the old wooden ones. Treated with an anticorrosive, these piles were supposed to last for many, many years. Twenty years later, the anticorrosive was worn away and in many places the steel itself was perforated: all the doings of sea urchins.

If they can do that to steel, one can imagine what these "living pin cushions" can do to the tender inner sole of a human foot. Likened to stepping on red-hot spikes, stepping on a sea urchin can result in excruciating pain that can last for hours. The puncture wounds they make can fester, and if the spines are not properly and completely removed they have to be taken out surgically. As if that is not bad enough, many species of sea urchins are venomous and can inject a poison strong enough to kill a person. The urchin injects its venom through fanglike jaws called pedicellariae. And should the brittle pedicellariae break off the urchin and get embedded in the skin, the venom flow continues until they are removed.

Also known as sea hedgehogs (the ancient Greeks used the same word for both sea urchins and hedgehogs), these symmetrical, and often beautiful, creatures hide in nooks and crannies along the sea coast or on the sea bottom. Some species "walk" along the bottom on their spines, whereas others propel themselves along an erratic course using their tube feet. These species will push their tube feet out, taking hold of something with the suckers attached to the feet. The retraction of the anchored tube foot pulls the body along.

In spite of their oddities and obvious dangers, sea urchins are sought after for their eggs, which are considered a delicacy in many parts of the world. They are especially popular in Malaya, Japan, South America, the

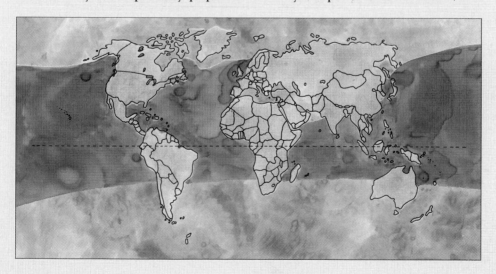

Mediterranean, and the Caribbean. In Barbados they are collected by naked divers using small hand nets—a rather risky operation.

Also rather risky is the eating of sea urchin roe, especially during mating season, because these eggs have been known to be toxic. All told, it is probably better to totally skirt these naughty and deadly urchins.

Name/Description

Sea urchins belong to the phylum Echinodermata. Closely related to starfish and sea cucumbers, sea urchins have rigid, globular, calcareous internal skeletons covered by a thin brittle shell of fused plates that form protuberances called tubercles. Attached to the tubercles are spines and pedicellariae. The spines vary in shape and length, but as a general rule the warmer the water is, the longer the spines are. The pedicellariae are small jointed rods with tiny, pincerlike organs that, when stimulated, clamp down and, in some species, envenom. On their undersurface, in addition to the mouth, are short spines and tube feet, used for slow locomotion on the sea floor. A water vascular system also aids in locomotion. There are numerous species, which vary in size from 1/2 inch to 18 inches. Sea urchins are found mostly in shallow waters among rocks, coral, and on sandy sea bottoms.

Toxicology

Injury: The sharp spines can cause painful puncture wounds. The brittle spines break easily and can become imbedded in a victim's skin.

Envenomization: Some species have poison glands on the pedicellariae. Sea urchin venom is usually syrupy and violet colored. Its toxic ingredients are unknown.

Ingestion: During mating season, some sea urchins produce a toxic substance that concentrates in the ovaries, making sea urchins dangerous to eat.

Symptoms

Injury: The small puncture wounds caused by the spines produce an immediate, intense pain that can last for hours; there may also be some

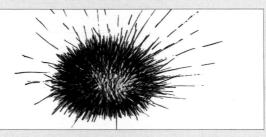

The spines of the sea urchin are strong enough to burrow through steel.

redness and swelling. Imbedded spines and improperly cleaned wounds can lead to secondary infections and gangrene.

Envenomization: In addition to the symptoms already described, envenomization causes nausea, faintness, numbness, weakness, muscular paralysis, respiratory distress, and in extreme cases, death.

Ingestion: Infection by toxic sea urchins causes gastric upset and in some cases, allergic reactions.

Treatment

Injury: Stingers should be completely removed, followed by cleaning of the wound with an antiseptic to prevent secondary infections. Imbedded stingers may need to be removed surgically. A doctor may prescribe an analgesic to help alleviate the pain.

Envenomization: Treatment for sea urchin envenomization is much the same as with Portuguese man-of-war stings (see p. 62). The pain usually diminishes within a few hours, but other symptoms may last three to four days. Although there have been fatalities, the envenomizations by sea urchins usually take a benign course and end without complications.

Prevention

• Be careful when wading in coastal waters where sea urchins are found. One should be especially careful of where he or she steps in these waters.

• Wear protective footwear and make sure it is strong, because sea urchin spines can penetrate sneakers and even rubber flippers.

SEA WASP

HOW IT GETS PEOPLE

Chironex fleckeri

HABITAT

CLIMATIC ZONE

RATING

General

The sea wasp is said to have killed almost as many people as have sharks off Australia's north coast since 1884, when such records were first begun. One of the world's most venomous animals, sea wasps are capable of killing a person faster than a massive heart attack. Its generic name, *Chironex fleckeri*, honors Dr. Hugo Flecker, an Australian physician who spent 20 years researching the cause of unexplained human fatalities in Australian waters.

Also known as the "box jelly" and the "fire medusa," the sea wasp may look graceful, even beautiful, in the water. It darts through the water by the propulsion of its long tentacles, which are as deadly as they are attractive. The sea wasp may have as many as 60 six-foot tentacles, each packed with millions of specialized nematocysts containing coiled,

Sea Wasp

barbed harpoonlike tubes that can immediately puncture and lock into a victim, releasing the instantly fatal venom into his or her skin.

After being stung while sitting in only knee-deep water in Townsville, Australia, Ann Richards shrieked and then collapsed on the beach. She had stopped breathing, and her face and limbs began turning black. A beach attendant doused the still-clinging tentacles with methylated spirits and gave Richards mouth-to-mouth resuscitation. She was taken to a hospital, where her bright red welts swelled, oozed, and burned for days. Luckily, Ann Richards survived, though she still bears hideous scars. When 13-year-old Kim Keeling was stung, she said she had been sure that a shark had attacked her—the pain was that intense. Those people were lucky but, unfortunately, the case of five-year-old Robin Hermann, who was stung by a sea wasp on the north coast of Australia in January 1986 and died before she could be pulled out of the water, is just as common.

Australia's lifeguards have found an effective, though rather unflattering, means of protection against the sea wasp. From December to April (the summer in Australia), when the sea wasp is most prevalent, lifeguards wear nylon panty hose, which the sea wasp's nematocysts

cannot penetrate. Many lifeguards also wear necklaces with plastic vials containing vinegar or acetic acid, which deactivate the nematocysts. Although this treatment may provide some relief, Australian jellyfish experts say it is far from a remedy.

Name/Description

A jellyfish of the class Scyphozoa, the adult sea wasp has a box–shaped bell that can fill a five–gallon bucket. Its long tentacles have millions of venomous nematocysts that discharge on contact with swimmers. Highly developed for a coelenterate (a member of the phylum Coelenterata), this jellyfish can easily maneuver around objects. Among the most venomous sea creatures known, it is found primarily along Australia's north coast.

Toxicology

Sea wasp venom is composed of a number of deadly toxins. If the venomous dose is large enough, the cardiotoxin can stop the heart of an adult in less than three minutes. If the dose is smaller, a neurotoxin can enter the brain and suppress breathing. The venom also contains a hemotoxin that can rupture the red blood cells and make the blood pressure drop precipitously. Even if the victim lives for a few days, he or she may later succumb because of kidney failure.

Symptoms

The first symptoms are an immediate, excruciating stinging sensation and seared reddened lines where the tentacles have come in contact with the skin. These contact points later turn into large, hardened weltlike lesions. In severe cases there will be violent shivering, vomiting, diarrhea, and a drop in blood pressure. Prostration, dizziness, circulatory failure, and respiratory distress precede a rapid death in a high percentage of cases. Most fatalities occur in children.

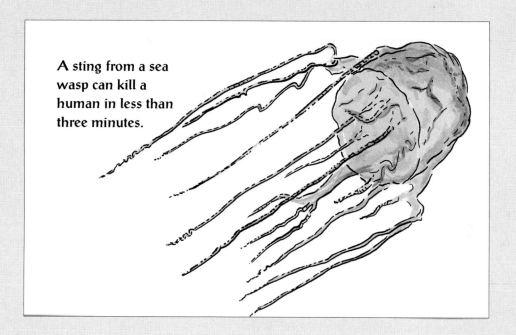

A sting from a sea wasp can kill a human in less than three minutes.

Treatment

Pour vinegar, methylated spirits, or diluted acetic acid over the clinging tentacles to inhibit any further venomous discharge. This procedure will also facilitate later removal of the tentacles. The affected extremity should be kept elevated. The victim should be covered with a blanket to guard against shock. When dealing with a sea wasp sting, time is of the essence; if the toxin enters the bloodstream, there may be only three minutes to act. It has been reported that a man in Queensland, Australia, died only 30 seconds after being stung. And although an antivenin is now available in Australia, there is rarely enough time to administer it. See Bites, Gorings, Maulings, and Shock, p. 112.

Prevention

• Avoid infested beaches and seas during sea wasp season.

SHARK

HOW IT GETS PEOPLE

Families: Charcarhinidae, Isuridae, and Shyrnidae

RATING

HOW IT GETS PEOPLE

CLIMATIC ZONE

CLIMATIC ZONE

HABITAT

HABITAT

General

The release of the movie *Jaws* in 1975 gave pause to many a beachgoer. The film, in which an ornery great white shark terrorizes a seaside resort community, alerted a broad audience to the dangers of shark attacks in dramatic (if not scientifically accurate) style. However, aquatic enthusiasts, such as surfers and divers, were already well aware of the dangers of the shark; they have been the overwhelming majority of its victims.

One such sportsman, Rodney Fox, an abalone diver from Adelaide, Australia, was bitten almost in half by a white shark. When finally hauled out of the water, his condition was desperate. His rib cage, lungs, and the upper part of his stomach were exposed, the flesh had been stripped from his arm, a lung was punctured, and his ribs were crushed. He was rushed to a nearby hospital, where it took delicate surgery and 462 stitches to save his life.

Another famous incident involved 100 divers participating in a spearfishing contest off the coast of San Francisco in January 1962. A great white shark had been spotted in the area, but contest officials decided to go ahead with the contest. The combination of fish wriggling in the water and the smell of blood was more than enough to arouse the interest of the great white. It grabbed Floyd Pair by the hips and legs. "It

shook me like a dog shakes a bone," he recalled. Pair struck back with his spear, jabbing it in the shark's snout, and was released. Prompt medical attention saved his legs and his life. But it is rare for a shark to attack in such a manner. A great white usually makes just a quick grab, takes a bite, and then throws the victim away like children discard toys with which they have grown tired.

Surfers are another group that have frequently been attacked by sharks. In 1980, Lewis Boren, surfing off the coast of Monterey, California, was the victim of one such attack. His surfboard was found cut almost in half by a bite from a 20-foot great white. Days later, his body washed ashore with bite marks closely matching those taken out of the board. Shark expert John McCosker had a theory about why the number of surfers who fell victim to sharks had risen dramatically in California waters. The Marine Mammal Protection Act, which was passed in 1972, resulted in a substantial increase in the number of harbor seals and California sea lions, the natural prey of the great white shark. At that time there was also a dramatic increase in the number of surfers. McCosker showed, through the use of underwater photography, how much a surfer paddling one of the new, shorter surfboards (five to six feet long) and wearing a wet suit resembles a sea lion swimming near the surface.

Especially vulnerable to shark attacks are survivors of boating accidents. One of the most famous incidents involved the crew of the USS *Indianapolis*. The *Indianapolis* was torpedoed by a Japanese submarine days after it had delivered to the American forces the atomic bomb that was to be dropped on Hiroshima. Because of the shroud of secrecy around the mission, rescue teams were not sent to look for the missing ship right away. When rescuers finally did reach the wreckage, the crew of the *Indianapolis* had been adrift in the shark-infested waters of the South Pacific for four days. Of the 1,199 men who managed to get off the foundering ship, only 316 survived the four-day nightmare in the water. Most of the 883 dead were eaten by sharks.

Shark

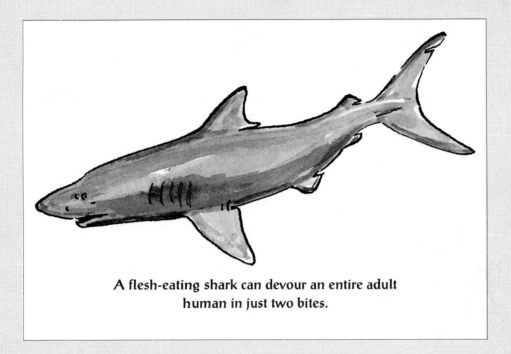

A flesh-eating shark can devour an entire adult human in just two bites.

Name/Description

Sharks are elasmobranch fish, their skeletons being made up of cartilage rather than bone. Torpedo shaped, they have lateral branchial clefts (side gill openings) and a tough, usually gray skin roughened by minute tubercles that serve as protective armor. With heterocercal tails (meaning that the spinal column ends in the tail's larger upper lobe), they have pectoral, pelvic, and two dorsal fins. Their teeth are razor sharp, daggerlike, and usually serrated. Although some sharks are as short as six inches, most of the species potentially dangerous to humans are 7 to 20 feet long.

Of the more than 250 species of sharks, only about 25 are dangerous to people, and these are in 2 of the 12 orders of sharks: Charcarhinoidiformes, which includes tiger and hammerhead sharks; and Isuriformes, which includes mako sharks and the great white (*Carcharodon charcharias*), one of the biggest and most dangerous sharks.

Injury

The jaw muscles of a shark are extremely powerful, and experiments carried out with a Snodgrass gnathodynamometer (a device that measures the strength of shark bites) at the Lerner Marine Lab in Bimini showed that they can bite down with a pressure of up to 19.6 tons per square inch. After biting, a shark usually shakes its victim fiercely, tearing out large amounts of flesh and leaving a very ragged wound that bleeds copiously. Death can result from shock, drowning, heart attack, or if the shark bites an artery, hemorrhaging. A lucky victim may have only a puncture wound.

Treatment

It is urgent to attempt to control the bleeding that results from a shark bite. Apply pressure to the wound with gauze or any clean fabric. A tourniquet may be necessary if a large artery was severed. After controlling the blood loss, lay the victim down, elevate the legs, and keep him or her warm. A doctor may give a tetanus shot and administer antibiotics after the wound has been treated. See also Bites, Gorings, Maulings, and Shock, p. 112.

Prevention

• Spearfishers should be especially cautious. They should remove their catch immediately and not haul it around.

Shark

- If confronted by a shark, at first remain as still as possible. Then swim away with slow, purposeful movements rather than erratic, panicky splashing.

- Avoid swimming when the underwater visibility is poor.

- Divers should wear dark clothing and should avoid carrying bright, shiny objects.

SPONGE

HOW IT GETS PEOPLE

Phylum: Porifera

HABITAT

CLIMATIC ZONE

CLIMATIC ZONE

RATING

General

When taking a bath, most people do not consider that they, as millions have for centuries, may be bathing with the lightweight skeleton of a porifera. Although somewhat rough when dry, these skeletons become soft when wet and have a characteristic elastic compressibility; thus they are able to absorb many times their own weight in water. But there are three families of sponges that one would not even want to touch, much less let run over one's naked body in the bathtub. Instead of coming out of the bathtub smelling sweet as a rose, a person could come out red and itchy and, within a few hours, covered with pus-filled blisters.

Although little is known and even less is understood about pori-feratoxins (toxic substances found in sponges), there are enough certified cases of sponge poisoning to warrant strict warnings to fishers, sponge divers, and recreational skin divers in certain areas. Because of their sessile habits (being permanently attached to a fixed base) and porous body structure, sponges are veritable hotels for other living sea creatures. They are known to house mollusks, worms, crustaceans, fish, algae, and even other sponges. Many of these inhabitants are poisonous as well.

Sponges feed by capturing microorganisms and organic debris as these different food sources move through their body's walls (it has been suggested that the sponges themselves may not produce toxic substances but rather absorb toxic substances from this food). It is speculated that sponges envenom by scratching a victim's skin with their spicules and then secreting venom into the wound. A typical example of envenomization, as cited by the noted animal expert Roger Caras, occurred among members of an underwater research group investigating Port Willunga Reef, St. Vincent Gulf, South Australia. One of the members of the party was diving with an aqualung at a depth of 30 feet in the vicinity of the reef when he spotted a large, dark sponge, bluish brown in color. It was about 18 inches square. The diver cut the sponge loose and surfaced with it. Other members of the team also handled the sponge freely aboard the boat. Later that night, the diver's hands grew sensitive and painful. Two days later his hands had become so swollen and blotchy that he could not even hold a pen to write. It took five days for his hands to recover. Others aboard the boat who had handled or

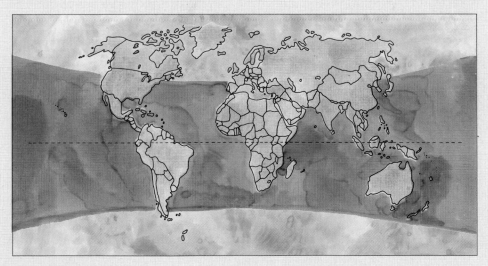

touched the sponge were also affected. One woman who touched it with her bare feet suffered extremely painful effects for several weeks and required extensive medical care. A nine-year-old boy suffered so much pain that he cried until the boat landed a few hours later. A photographer in the group handled the specimen freely and felt no immediate effects. The next day, however, the itching and pain started and spread to parts of his body that had not even come in contact with the sponge. Today, sponges remain mysterious, and sometimes dangerous, creatures of the deep.

Name/Description

Sponges are plantlike, multicellular, predominantly marine animals of simple and loose organization. Some 5,000 species of sponges belong to the phylum Porifera (the name refers to the many pores through which water circulates into the sponge's internal chamber), but only three families are dangerous: the Desmacidonidae, found in the West Indies and the western Atlantic; the Haliclonidae, also of the West Indies; and the Tedaniidae, found in most coastal waters of the United States.

Sponges have unique supportive skeletal systems made up of spiny spicules composed of calcium, silicon, or organic matter. They obtain food by propelling water through tiny pores in the body wall, thus capturing microorganisms and organic debris. Because they have no digestive tract, digestion is intracellular. Sponges constitute a rich source of biologically active substances, including antibiotic and toxic materials.

Toxicology

Toxic sponges secrete or discharge substances that are irritating on contact. But how the toxins are produced, their chemical makeup, and their location in the sponge is largely unknown.

Symptoms

There is disagreement as to whether symptoms of sponge envenomization are the result of chemical or mechanical irritation. Most evidence

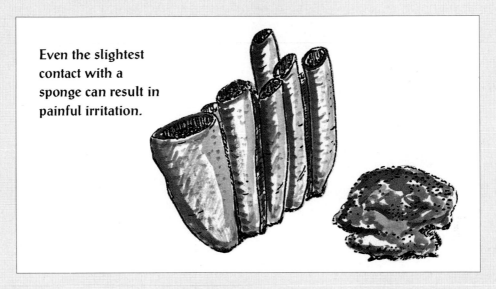

Even the slightest contact with a sponge can result in painful irritation.

points to chemical intoxication, the toxin being a primitive venom. Within a few minutes the victim feels intense burning and itching around the affected area, then redness of the skin develops, followed by swelling and a feeling of stiffness in the finger joints. Within a few hours blisters may develop over the affected area. The symptoms usually disappear after a few days, but if inadequately treated, they can persist for months.

Treatment

Wash the affected area as soon as possible with soap and water. Place antiseptic dressings over any open cuts. Soothing lotions such as calamine or over-the-counter cortisone creams may relieve the itching. A doctor may prescribe an anesthetic cream, such as benzocaine, to relieve the pain.

Prevention

• Wear diving gloves and wet suits in sponge-infested waters.

• Avoid even the slightest contact with a sponge .

STINGRAY

HOW IT GETS PEOPLE

Family: Dasyatidae

HABITAT

CLIMATIC ZONE

RATING

General

Just like the sports car that is named for it, the stingray is sleek, streamlined, and quite hazardous if not handled with caution. This dangerous fish is the cause of one the most common and painful envenomizations in the marine environment. Most stingray victims are bathers who inadvertently tread on them in shallow water. Commercial fishers compose the second largest group of victims. They are usually stung by stingrays hidden among their catch. James "Coolidge" Judah, who fishes out of Sebastian, Florida, has been stung more than 20 times. He says, "The pain is just terrible, as bad as anything you'll want to feel. It'll make a grown man holler."

And then there are amateur fishers, such as Eric Sharp. A freelance writer, Sharp, out of self-proclaimed "macho conceit," tried to save a 49-cent fishing line by attempting to take the hook out of the stingray his son had unintentionally caught. This maneuver earned him a stab wound in the hand that landed him in the hospital. He suffered hours of unremitting pain that even Demerol, a very strong painkiller, could not relieve. A doctor told Sharp that even the strongest of painkillers falls short of relieving the pain of a stingray wound; simply put, the doctor told Sharp, "You're going to hurt."

Not only did he hurt, but he also lost the use of his hand for a week. Horrified, he watched his hand swell until, as he describes it, it was "thicker than the Miami telephone book." This injury would be bad enough for anyone, but for a writer it was particularly debilitating. Unable to write or type but intrigued by the injury he had just sustained, he set about interviewing stingray victims and listened to their stories. He met a dancer whose career had been ended by a stingray wound that had destroyed her calf muscle; a fisher who had to spend a month in bed after he was skewered by the fish and could just barely hobble around months after the incident; and a businessman from Atlanta who, two years after the incident, had no feeling in the area where he had been stung.

People who have been stung by stingrays say they will never be able to forget it—most seem at a loss for words to describe the pain. Toxin expert Dr. Findlay–Russell, says that stingray venom is unbelievably and unbearably painful. Furthermore, even without envenomization the

barbed spines of the stingray—so sharp that American Indians and Australian aborigines used them as spearheads—leave behind jagged wounds that are quite gruesome in themselves.

Name/Description

Stingrays belong to the family Dasyatidae. Somewhat resembling birds of prey in flight, stingrays have flattened bodies and winglike pectoral fins. They have a long, sharp barbed dorsal spine near the base of their whiplike tail. The spine harbors a thick stinger that is barbed along the edges and is covered by a skin sheath. Rays bury themselves in muddy bottoms, where only their eyes, which are on top of their head, protrude from the sandy floor. They feed on worms, crustaceans, and mollusks, which they excavate from the bottom with their pectoral fins. Normally, rays are about six feet long and three feet wide. The biggest species is the Australian giant stingray (*Dasyotis brevicaudata*), measuring 14 feet long, 7 feet wide, and weighing as much as 750 pounds.

Toxicology

The stingray uses its stinger almost exclusively as a defense mechanism, attacking only if provoked. This fact, however, does not make their stings any less painful or dangerous. When stepped on or otherwise provoked, the stingray lashes its formidable tail from side to side or up and down. Without a clear target, chances are good that the stinger will miss the intruder's foot or just strike a glancing blow. But if it connects, the stingray has been known to drive its spine deep into a wooden plank or completely through a victim's limb. Even if a victim is not en-venomed, he or she can still get a serious secondary infection from parts of the stinger sheath that may be left in the wound.

Symptoms

Because of the jagged retrorse barbs on the stinging spines, the stingray leaves deep, ragged lacerations that bleed profusely. Within minutes of

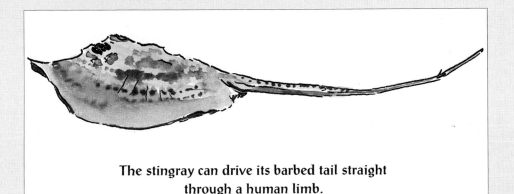

The stingray can drive its barbed tail straight through a human limb.

being stung, there is extreme pain. If envenomed, there will be cramping, abdominal pain, vomiting, difficulty in breathing, and marked vasoconstriction (narrowing of the blood vessels), which may send the victim into shock, coma, or in rare cases, death. Stingray venom is thought to have a direct effect on the human heart muscle as well.

Treatment

Treatment for a stingray stab wound is similar to that for scorpionfish envenomization. Immerse the affected appendage or limb in hot water (not more than 120° F) for an hour or so. The venom is heat labile and is quickly neutralized. Parts of the stinging spine and any membranes should be carefully removed to prevent secondary infection of the wound. A doctor may give pentazocine lactate for pain, as well as a local anesthetic, antihistaminic compound, or tetanus.

Prevention

- Bathers in areas where stingrays are common should shuffle their feet or probe ahead of themselves with a stick to alert unwary stingrays to their presence. The disturbance should be enough to encourage the ray to seek a less traveled spot.

SWORDFISH

HOW IT GETS PEOPLE

Xiphias gladius

HABITAT

CLIMATIC ZONE

CLIMATIC ZONE

RATING

General

The phrase "to die by the sword" evokes images of knightly jousts or swashbuckling adventures of the kind one might see in an Errol Flynn movie. But a man sailing on in the River Severn near Worcester, England, who was "struck and absolutely received his death wound" by a swordfish, was afforded no chivalric honors.

Although swordfish do not deliberately attack humans, they have been known for centuries to attack the hull of ships, earning them the nickname the "rhinoceros of the sea." The incidents have occurred all over the world. The Associated Press reported that the 30-ton *Genyo Maru* had been rammed by a swordfish amidship and was sinking, stranding a 15-man crew at sea. The research submarine *Alvin* was attacked by a 200-pound swordfish while surveying a sea bed at a depth of 1,800 feet off the coast of Georgia. After piercing a joint in the external hull, the fish was unable to extricate itself and was carried to the surface with the submarine. A small ship off the coast of Brazil was struck with such force one night that the helmsman could hardly keep her on course. Another ship, off the Azores Islands, was hit so hard that the crew thought she had struck a rock. Preserved in the British Museum is a timber from a ship that had been penetrated to a depth of 22 inches by a swordfish.

For centuries, seamen have been finding broken-off swords in the hull of their ships. When the whaler *Fortune* reached harbor at Plymouth, Massachusetts, in 1826, she had a sword in her hull that penetrated a copper sheathing, four inches of board, a foot of solid oak, two and a half inches of hard oak ceiling, and the head of an oil cask.

One of the reasons the swordfish is able to inflict so much damage on ships is the speed at which it swims. Using its long snout as a cutwater, the swordfish can swim at speeds of up to 60 miles per hour, enabling it to strike with incredible force. Suppose a rather lazy 600-pound swordfish was swimming at the leisurely rate of 10 miles per hour and rammed a ship. It would be striking with the force of one-third of a ton per square inch. And if the ship were traveling toward the fish at

the same speed, the force of impact would be four and a half tons per square inch.

Even though the swordfish has inflicted serious damage on boats, its preferred victims are other fish. Swimming around shoals (shallow areas and sandbars), they thrash their sword about, beating the fish, later eating the dead and stunned fish at their leisure. The swordfish is popular commercially—20,000 swordfish are caught off North American waters each year—even though the discovery of mercury in swordfish in the 1970s led to tighter controls being placed on its sale in the United States. However, recent studies have shown that the high levels of mercury in swordfish are not necessarily connected with industrial pollution; the same levels have been found in museum specimens collected decades ago.

Name/Description

The swordfish (*Xiphias gladius*) is a beautifully streamlined fish, the upper jaw of which is carried forward into a swordlike beak, flattened from top to bottom. Although some specimens measure up to 14 feet long and weigh up to 1,000 pounds, most swordfish average a length of 6 to 11 feet and weigh between 100 and 300 pounds. The front dorsal fin is high, narrow at the base, and curves backward. When the swordfish swims near the surface, this fin cleaves the water much like the fin of a shark, for which it is often mistaken. The first anal fin is fairly large, but both the second dorsal fin and the second anal fin are very small and set far back. The narrow body (flat from side to side) is a dark purple blue on the back, changing to silver gray on the underside. The "sword" is black above and paler on the underside. Rather solitary, the swordfish not only swims swiftly, but it can also make enormous leaps out of the water—making it a popular game fish.

Swordfish prefer warmer seas, but they have been found in such areas as the British Isles in the summer and autumn, when oceanic currents brings warmer water farther north than usual.

Swordfish

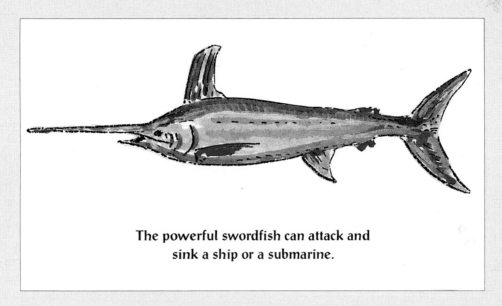

The powerful swordfish can attack and sink a ship or a submarine.

Injury

A swordfish, which can hit a stationary object with tremendous force, could certainly go through a human pretty easily. Although there are no records of deliberate swordfish attacks on humans, many people are injured while sportfishing. When hauling a swordfish aboard boats, many sportfishers fall victim to the wild thrashing about of their catch—and that snout can make nasty gashes and puncture wounds. Most victims are left with large, gaping wounds, and as with any serious injury, they can go into shock.

Symptoms and Treatment

See Bites, Gorings, Maulings, and Shock, p. 112.

Prevention

• Sportfishers should be cautious when hauling in a swordfish.

WEEVER FISH

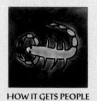

HOW IT GETS PEOPLE

Trachinus draco, T. araneus, T. radiatus, and T. vipera

HABITAT

CLIMATIC ZONE

CLIMATIC ZONE

RATING

General

Although European fishers have known of the poisonous nature of weever fish since ancient times, they still risk painful stings to catch them for their extremely high commercial value. But sometimes the price can be too high, for the sting of a weever fish produces such unbearable agony that one fisher amputated his own finger in an attempt to relieve the pain.

The weever (also spelled weaver) is probably a corruption of the Anglo-Saxon word *wivre*, which means "viper." However, unlike the vipers found slithering on land, the weever uses its spines, rather than fangs, to strike. In England they are also known as "sea dragons." But by any name, weevers are certainly the most venomous fish in temperate and northern seas.

Weever fish

Most people are stung by weevers when handling the nets in which the fish are caught or when preparing the fish for market—even when dead they can inflict painful stings. Although some countries have enacted legislation requiring the removal of the venomous spines before marketing, this practice is far from universal. Highly sought after for their firm white flesh and excellent taste, tons of weevers are marketed in Europe each year. They are especially prized in France, where they are considered a great delicacy.

In spite of their extensive range, weevers have rather sedentary habits and spend most of their time partially buried in mud or sand, with only their head exposed. Intermittently, they will dart out to capture prey, then settle back down into the sea bottom. At rest the dorsal fin is depressed, but when aroused this fin is erect and the opercular fins (on the bony covering protecting the gills) are expanded. Unlike the venomous stingray and scorpionfish, which are often reluctant to attack, it does not take much to provoke a weever. The mere presence of a hand or a foot in its territory is enough to spark this pugnacious piscine to confrontation. They move very swiftly, and even

the slightest touch on their body may cause them to strike with severity and accuracy.

Weevers can be a terror to fishers in shallow, sandy areas who are trying to catch other, less risky, fish. And incidents of bizarre reactions to weever fish stings are numerous and varied. Fishers have been known to hammer tholes (metal pins that serve as fulcrums for oars) into weever wounds to deaden the pain. Other victims have plunged affected appendages into fire to "kill" the pain. One fisher was seen wrapping his wound with vinegar–soaked paper and lighting it in desperate hope of relief.

Name/Description

The four species of weever fish are *Trachinus draco*, *T. araneus*, *T. radiatus*, and *T. vipera*. They are small (10 to 20 inches long) marine fish of the family Trachinidae. Weevers are distinguished by eyes near the tops of their head and long, soft dorsal and anal fins that have spines. In addition, they have two opercular spines located on either side of the head. Each spine has its own venom-producing tissue, consisting of large pink cells filled with a fine granular substance. Weevers are found at the bottom of the sea, near shrimp beds, or in flat, sandy, or muddy bays where they can partially bury themselves. In spring and early summer, weevers migrate to shallow waters to spawn. They feed on crustaceans, annelids (worms and leeches), and small fish. If approached, weevers can become quite aggressive.

Toxicology

Not much is known about weever fish venom, but it is thought to contain peptides, enzymes, and a variety of vasoactive compounds (substances that affect the blood vessels).

Symptoms

Symptoms include instantaneous pain, which is usually described as burning, stabbing, or crushing.

One fisher amputated his own finger to relieve the pain of a weever fish sting.

There may develop an urgency to urinate. The pain spreads through-out the entire affected limb and becomes progressively more intense, causing the victim to scream in anguish. There will be numbness around the wound, swelling, redness, delirium, respiratory distress, convulsions, and in rare cases, death. Even with very mild envenomization, the severe pain may last for hours, and there may be secondary infections leading to gangrene.

Treatment

There is no antivenin for the venom of the weever. Morphine is inef-fective. A doctor may administer intravenous calcium gluconate or meperidine, which may be effective in alleviating the pain.

Prevention

- Stay out of water where there may be weever fish. Even shuffling the feet or prodding ahead with a stick will most likely provoke the weever fish rather than drive it away.

- Never handle a weever fish, even a dead one, without wearing a pair of thick gloves.

APPENDIX I:
Bites, Gorings, Maulings, and Shock

One does not have to be lost in the African bush or wandering through the jungle to be ferociously mauled or bitten. In just the past few years three people were attacked by animals in British safari parks, a young zookeeper in New York was killed by tigers, a model in Canada was mauled by a tiger during a photo shoot, and a 24-year-old park naturalist was attacked and eaten by a bear in Glacier National Park, Canada. Every year in the United States more than one million people are bitten severely enough by animals to require hospital attention.

A dog bite can produce lacerations, destruction of soft tissue, and even compound fractures. If a 30-pound dog can inflict that much damage, imagine the damage a 750-pound grizzly bear can inflict. Contrary to the popular saying, the bite of most animals is worse than their bark; nonetheless, bites are often one of their lesser threats. For example, many large animals do not bother to bite their victims at all, preferring instead to trample or kneel on them, thus crushing them and causing severe internal injuries. The tusks, horns, and antlers of other beasts can gore and rip open the body, causing lung damage which can result in pneumothorax (an accumulation of air or gas in the pleural cavity), perforation of the intestines, bleeding from the liver and spleen, and the loss of eyes or ears. In addition, all bites and gorings carry a heavy risk of infection from the bacteria, viruses, and other microorganisms that may be present in the attacking animal's mouth or that may have contaminated its paws, horns, or claws. Virtually all animal injuries require tetanus prophylactic (protecting against disease) measures, and the threat of rabies must also be considered.

The following is a sample of first aid measures that should be taken until a victim can receive professional medical care.

Wounds
For gaping abdominal wounds or profuse bleeding from an extremity,
- cover the wound with a clean cloth, gauze, or sheet dressing;

- apply direct pressure to try to stop the bleeding;
- keep the victim calm, warm, and prone. Keep reassuring him or her.

For a puncture wound in the chest,

- cover the wound with a clean dressing, then wrap and knot a rope, belt, tie, or scarf around the chest to help keep the wound closed;
- keep the victim calm, warm, and prone. Keep reassuring him or her.

For a puncture wound caused by the bite of a dog or a small animal,

- immediately clean the wound, using antiseptics if they are available;
- apply a clean dressing;
- control any bleeding by pressing firmly on the dressing.

Shock

Apart from the aforementioned injuries, a victim of a serious attack may also go into shock. A term that many people use informally, *shock*, in medical terms, is a profoundly disturbing, often fatal condition characterized by a failure of the circulatory system to maintain an adequate blood supply to vital organs. It can be caused by severe injury, blood loss, or disease.

Shock is a state in which perfusion (passage of blood to the vessels) and the blood flow to peripheral tissues are inadequate to sustain life because of insufficient levels of carbon dioxide in the blood or maldistribution of blood flow. Shock is associated with diminished peripheral circulation, hypotension (abnormally low blood pressure), and oliguria (diminished urine output).

Other symptoms are lethargy, confusion, and somnolence (unnatural drowsiness). The victim's hands and feet are cold, moist, and often cyanotic (having a bluish discoloration as a result of insufficient oxygen in the blood), and his or her pulse is weak and rapid.

Untreated, shock is usually fatal. Treatment depends on the cause, the presence of a preexisting or complicating illness, and the time between onset and diagnosis. The victim should be kept warm, with legs raised slightly to improve circulation. The victim's airway and ventilation should be checked, and respiratory assistance should be given if necessary. The head of a shock victim should be turned to one side to prevent choking on his or her own vomit.

APPENDIX II:
Ciguatera Poisoning

Every year, people from all over the world, yearning for a respite from the dog-eat-dog world, vacation in the tropics. Far from polluted air, junk food, and traffic jams, they savor exotic, healthy fruits, vegetables, and seafood. However, many of these vacationers fall victim to ciguatera poisoning, the most common fish poisoning in the world. A result of what might be called the "fish-eat-fish" world, ciguatera poisoning is caused in most instances by eating a poisonous fish that has eaten a poisonous fish that has eaten a poisonous microorganism.

Eating any kind of fish in the tropics is somewhat akin to playing Russian roulette, because any one of more than 400 species could be safely edible on one beach and only a few miles down the coast, toxic enough to kill a person. Even when the poison is not fatal, it can result in some serious and rather bizarre symptoms, such as the "dry-ice" sensation, a paradoxical sensory disturbance in which hot feels cold and cold feels hot. Four weeks after a naval officer was poisoned by eating a toxic amberjack, he was observed unconsciously blowing on his ice cream, which he said was burning his tongue.

The name *ciguatera* derives from a Spanish word for a different disease, brought on by ingesting *cigua*, or poisonous snails. The real source of ciguatera poisoning—identified only in 1979—is Gambierdiscus, a toxic, microscopic unicellular organism that lives in the ecosystems (primarily coral) near the blue-green algae upon which plant-eating bottom-dwelling fish live. These herbivorous (plant-eating) fish are in turn consumed by larger, carnivorous fish, in the flesh and internal organs of which the toxin becomes concentrated. The toxin does not affect the flavor of the fish, and there are no cooking or processing procedures that can reduce or eliminate it.

Appendix II

Toxicology

The potent nerve toxin ciguera is unaffected by freezing, storage, or heat. It gives no unusual taste, color, or odor to the fish. The most toxic parts of the fish are, in order, the liver, the intestines, the testes, the ovaries, and the muscles.

Symptoms

Symptoms of ciguatera poisoning vary greatly with the amount of fish eaten and the part of the fish eaten. There are two groups of ciguatera poisoning symptoms—gastrointestinal, which affects the stomach and intestines, and neurological, which affects the nerves. Acute abdominal pain, nausea, and vomiting usually occur about six hours after ingestion. These symptoms disappear in six to eight hours and are followed by a second set of symptoms: numbness and a tingling, burning sensation in the extremities—the previously discussed "dry ice." Other symptoms may include muscle soreness and joint pain. Headache, chills, cramps, itchiness, loss of motor coordination, and dizziness also may follow. In severe poisonings, these symptoms progress to foaming at the mouth, muscular paralysis, dyspnea (difficulty in breathing), and convulsions. Death may occur from convulsions or respiratory failure anytime from 1 to 24 hours after ingesting the poison. Ciguatera poisoning is fatal for up to 20% of its victims.

Treatment

Treatment of ciguatera poisoning is largely symptomatic, and there are no specific antidotes. Treatment should first concentrate on eliminating the poison from the body by use of emetics or gastric lavage. A doctor may prescribe opiates for pain and diarrhea as well as Atropine, which may relieve cardiovascular pains and symptoms. Although most symptoms will disappear in a few days, in severe poisonings there may be residual weakness and sensory changes that can persist for weeks or even years.

Prevention

No matter what the locals say, there is no way to determine if a fish is ciguatoxic. When traveling to faraway places, it is probably a good idea to eat fish only at reputable restaurants and hotels and not to buy it fresh.

FURTHER READING

Caras, Roger. *Dangerous to Man.* South Hackensack, NJ: Stoeger, 1975.

Ellis, Richard. *The Book of Sharks: A Complete Illustrated Natural History of the Sharks of the World.* San Diego: Harcourt Brace Jovanovich, 1983.

Greenberg, Idaz, and Jerry Greenberg. *Sharks and Other Dangerous Sea Creatures.* Miami: Seahawk Press, 1981.

Grzimek, Bernard. *Grzimek's Animal Life Encyclopedia.* New York: Macmillan, 1984.

Hauser, Hilary. *Skin Diver Magazine's Book of Fishes.* Glen Cove, NY: PBC International, 1984.

Helm, Thomas. *Dangerous Sea Creatures: A Complete Guide to Hazardous Marine Life.* New York: Funk & Wagnalls, 1976.

Nelson, Joseph S. *Fishes of the World.* New York: Wiley, 1984.

Oxford Scientific Films Staff. *Jellyfish and Other Sea Creatures.* New York: Putnam, 1982.

Walker, Charlotte. *Fish and Shellfish.* Los Angeles: Price Stern, 1984.

Whitfield, Philip, ed. *Macmillan Illustrated Animal Encyclopedia.* New York: Macmillan, 1984.

Wood, Gerald. *Animal Facts and Feats.* New York: Sterling, 1977.

INDEX

Index

Missy Allen is a writer and photographer whose works have appeared in *Time*, *Geo*, *Vogue*, *Paris-Match*, *Elle*, and many European publications. Allen holds a master's degree in education from Boston University. Before her marriage to Michel Peissel, she worked for the Harvard School of Public Health and was director of admissions at Harvard's Graduate School of Arts and Sciences.

Michel Peissel is an anthropologist, explorer, inventor, and author. He has studied at the Harvard School of Business, Oxford University, and the Sorbonne. Called "the last true adventurer of the 20th century," Peissel discovered 14 Mayan sites in the eastern Yucatán at the age of 21 and was elected the youngest member of the New York Explorers Club. He is also one of the world's foremost experts on the Himalayas, where he has led 14 major expeditions. Peissel has also written 14 books, published in 83 editions in 15 countries.

When not found in their fisherman's house in Cadaqués, Spain, with their two young children, Peissel and Allen can be found trekking across the Himalayas or traveling in Central America.

ACKNOWLEDGMENTS

The authors would like to thank Lisa Bateman for her editorial assistance; Brian Rankin for his careful typing; and Linnie Greason, Heather Moulton, and Luis Abiega for so kindly allowing their lives to be infiltrated by these creepy crawlies and ferocious fauna.

CREDIT

All the original watercolor illustrations are by Michel Peissel, and the geographic distribution maps are by Diana Blume.